THE KING AND THE KINGDOM

THE KING AND THE KINGDOM

Leslie Brown

MOWBRAYS
LONDON & OXFORD

Copyright © L. W. Brown

First published 1988
by A.R. Mowbray & Co. Ltd,
Saint Thomas House, Becket Street,
Oxford, OX1 1SJ

Typeset by Getset (BTS) Ltd., Oxford
Printed in Great Britain by
Cox and Wyman Ltd., Reading

British Library Cataloguing in Publication Data

Brown, Leslie, *1912* –
    The king and the kingdom. — (Mowbray's
    popular Christian paperbacks).
    1. Lent — Meditations
    I. Title
    232'.34   BV85

ISBN 0-264-67141-4

Introduction

This book offers seven meditations on the Gospels provided in the Alternative Service Book for Ash Wednesday and the six Sundays of Lent. The themes suggested in that book are followed here. The hope is that each chapter will provide material for reflection for a week.

Each chapter is prefaced by the story of someone I have known who seems to embody the theme of the week. I have limited the field by describing only people I have known myself. Probably many readers can think of people of their own acquaintance, who would illustrate the point equally well. It would be quite a helpful Lent exercise to remember them, and be grateful for them. I realise that nearly all the people I describe could serve also as examples of some other theme in the book, for temptation, suffering and conflict are only aspects of the experience of all who try to follow our Lord.

The younger Churches are living in the same generations of faith, first, second, third or fourth as the Christians for whom the New Testament books were written. The illustrations I have used are mostly drawn from the Church in India or Uganda. I hope they will not only clarify the New Testament experience but also help us to respond appreciatively and gratefully to the witness of the younger Churches in the Anglican family, which the Lambeth Conference in the summer of 1988 will bring vividly to our attention.

The story of Bishop Festo Kivengere on p. 67 is reprinted from his book, *I Love Idi Amin*, with his permission and that of the publisher, Messrs Marshall Pickering. A sentence from Malcolm Muggeridge's book, *Something Beautiful for God*, is quoted with the permission of Messrs Collins Publishers. I am grateful for these permissions.

Because of impaired vision I could not have written this book without the help of my wife, and of Sue Cunliffe, who has turned tapes into typescript and helped me revise and edit the result. Peter May has also helped me with checking scripts and references, and I am grateful.

Leslie Brown

Contents

Ash Wednesday

Jesus told a parable, which was aimed at those who were sure of their own goodness and looked down on everyone else. 'Two men went up to the temple to pray, one a Pharisee and the other a tax gatherer. The Pharisee stood up and prayed thus; "I thank thee, O God, that I am not like the rest of men, greedy, dishonest, adulterous; or, for that matter, like this tax gatherer. I fast twice a week; I pay tithes on all that I get." But the other kept his distance and would not even raise his eyes to heaven, but beat upon his breast, saying, "O God, have mercy on me, sinner that I am." It was this man, I tell you, and not the other, who went home acquitted of his sins. For everyone who exalts himself will be humbled; and whoever humbles himself will be exalted.'

(Luke 18. 9-14 NEB)

Very few people have ever heard of Julia Caroline Potts. Mrs Potts lived alone in a single room above a bookmaker's shop off one of the main streets of Portsmouth. The only way of visiting her was to go

1

through the shop, up a flight of stairs to her door at the top. She was frequently visited by the curates of the nearby parish church. We went not only as a pastoral duty but because we positively enjoyed seeing her. Some of the young girls of the parish also went in daily to see the old lady. They shopped for her and sometimes did her cooking. Probably in any case there was very little cooking to be done.

I do not know Mrs Potts' background. She must have moved to this room in her old age. She was eighty-five when I knew her, and of course at that time there were not the social services which today would be responsible for caring for the elderly.

Mrs Potts generally dressed in heavy woollen clothes. She was short with white hair and a rather pinched face. She usually sat in a large, straight arm-chair, but for most of the time I knew her she was in bed because she had a broken leg and could not move about. The most remarkable feature of Mrs Potts was her eyes. They were very ordinary eyes but they sparkled with intelligence and good humour and interest in all she heard from her visitors about the outside world. She made sensible comments on any news items she was told, but she never pried into other people's affairs and she never gossiped. If she had anything to say it was, in my experience, in-variably kind.

Mrs Potts was semi-literate. I do not believe she could write. She could read but she read only one book. The Bible was always close at hand and she would often discuss with her curate visitors a passage she had been reading that day. I vividly remember one occasion when I went through the bookmaker's

shop and up the stairs and knocked on Mrs Potts'
door. When I told her who was knocking she at once
called me in. She was sitting up in bed with a look of
great pleasure on her face. Her spectacles and her
Bible were on the bed and she said, 'Oh, Mr Brown,
I'm so glad to see you. I wanted to say to somebody –
what *would* we do without the Holy Spirit.'

Mrs Potts' very simple faith irradiated the whole of
her life. I do not believe that she ever found it necessary to humble herself like the tax collector in the story
Jesus told. She certainly never prided herself or congratulated herself on her goodness. I do not think she
thought about herself at all. She saw God's hand in
everything that happened and she was happy to feel
that he was there in the room with her sharing her life.
I am sure if you had said anything to her about her
goodness she would have repudiated the idea
instantly and said that she was sometimes a grumpy
old woman who felt sorry for herself, but I do not
think that would have been abasing herself deliberately. She accepted herself as she was but she had no
time to think about it because she was so filled with
the recollection of God's goodness to her and, as was
evident by the remark I have quoted, by the presence
and power of the Holy Spirit.

I would often call on Mrs Potts when I was feeling
tired or despondent about the work I was doing in the
parish because to meet this lady, very simple, un-
educated in the usual sense of the word but really
understanding the way God worked, was an inspir-
ation and encouragement and a joy. Every week at
staff meeting her name would be mentioned in the list
of sick people to be visited and reported on. When

Mrs Potts' name was mentioned there would be a grin of recollection from several of the curates who had all been cheered and amused during the week by her constant happiness and good humour.

Anyone who has thought at all about his own nature or human nature as a whole can easily understand Luke's report of the story Jesus told. Two men go into the great courtyard of the Temple to pray. It was rather like the cloister of a monastery or a court or quadrangle of a college. The central space was paved but free of any buildings. The Pharisee goes and stands near the front and prays, facing the Holy of Holies. Perhaps Luke is saying that he doesn't pray. He just gives expression to his own satisfaction with himself and his spiritual standing in the eyes of God, and turns it into a thanksgiving. The other man, a tax man in the service of the Roman Government, doesn't make any pretentions at all to importance. He stands near the back. Luke says that this man, conscious of his own sinfulness in the sight of God, simply asks for God's mercy, and that he went down to his house righteous, accepted by God, rather than the other man.

Both men were acutely aware of their own feelings. The Pharisee was happy at his own importance and the way people recognised him, and was satisfied with the way he carried out his spiritual duties. In his self-satisfaction he thanked God that he was not like other men or even like the tax collector fellow standing at the back. It appears that he was not so much aware of God as of himself. The tax man was also conscious of himself and his own needs. But he was aware of God and he took his sense of need straight to God and was heard.

The Pharisees have, on the whole, a very bad Press in the Gospels. They were certainly not, as a class, bad men. Their whole life was spent in the service of their religion which was closely connected with their sense of nationhood and their identity as the people of God. They were sometimes tempted to think that they were the only true people of God left. The Roman and Greek cultures had influenced many of their compatriots. The priestly families of the Sadducees, the virtual rulers of the country under the Romans, were certainly not fully observant Jews. The Pharisees spent a great deal of time in the study rooms connected with the synagogues poring over the scriptures. They had produced many learned teachers and rabbis who knew the Law of Moses and all the immense volume of observances and regulations which stemmed from it. They were learned in the opinion of the rabbis which formed the precedents for their judgements. They said the routine daily prayers. They fasted on the appointed days. They went to Jerusalem to the Temple on the great national festivals, and they gave a tenth of all they had for God's service even to tithing the herbs they used in the kitchen. For many of them all this had become an end in itself, a source of pride and parade. They were proud of being religious and proud of the strictness of their observance. This brought with it a sense of judgement and condemnation of those who were not as they were. It was this that constituted their sin. The Gospels are full of stories of the encounters of Jesus with the Pharisees, how they attended his meetings or watched him while he was healing, and all the time, the Gospel writers say, not in order to be instructed, but in order to catch him on some point which could lead to his condemnation. They had great controversies with him about healing sick people on the Sabbath day and doing other things which it was not lawful to do on that day. Jesus replied sharply saying that they knew perfectly well that if one of them had a domestic animal fallen into an open well on the Sabbath day he would certainly pull the animal out. Was it not therefore even more the will of God that he should heal a sick man on the Sabbath day? Jesus' observance of the Sabbath was one of the great points of controversy. The Pharisee in the story must have been one of the strict and critical kind. But there were certainly many other Pharisees who were humble men of God, people like Nicodemus and Joseph of Arimathea who are mentioned in the Gospel story. Undoubtedly there were many others for whom religion had not become their God, but who humbly tried to find the will of the God of their fathers. It seems that what is being condemned by Jesus is the human tendency to make religion an end in itself, a god, and to regard the fulfilment of religious obligations as the only way of doing God's will. This is dangerous because it can easily lead to pride in one's own achievement as well as to an absurdly limited understanding of God.

We do not know what made the tax man feel so guilty. He did not even stand in the normal attitude of prayer with his eyes lifted up to heaven and his hands stretched out in praising God. His head was cast

6

down, his whole appearance was dejected and all he could do was to ask for God's mercy. It would seem likely that he was not confessing failure to fulfil the obligations and regulations of the law, but that he was convicted in his heart of some moral failure for which he could not forgive himself and was afraid that God could not either. He was conscious of himself as a man who had sinned and threw himself on the mercy of God as the only way he knew in which that sin could be removed.

Luke tells us that this man went down to his house justified rather than the other. His use of the Greek word translated 'justified' in the older English versions is interesting because it links directly with one of the main themes of Paul's teaching. Luke was a close friend of Paul and accompanied him on some of his missionary journeys. Clearly he had understood and accepted the teaching of Paul that when a human being confronts God he has to put his trust and confidence in God's mercy alone, not in any achievement of his own. Paul expresses his own position very clearly:

> Though I myself have reason for confidence in the flesh also. If any other man thinks he has reason for confidence in the flesh I have more: circumcised on the eighth day, of the people of Israel, of the tribe of Benjamin, a Hebrew born of Hebrews; as to the law a Pharisee, as to zeal a persecutor of the church, as to righteousness under the law blameless. But whatever gain I had, I counted as loss for

the sake of Christ. Indeed I count everything as loss because of the surpassing
worth of knowing Christ Jesus my Lord.
For his sake I have suffered the loss of all
things, and count them as refuse, in order
that I may gain Christ and be found in him,
not having a righteousness of my own,
based on law, but that which is through
faith in Christ, the righteousness from God
that depends on faith; that I may know him
and the power of his resurrection, and may
share his sufferings, becoming like him in
his death, that if possible I may attain the
resurrection from the dead.

(Philippians 3. 4-11 RSV)

Paul spells out his position even more clearly in the
letter to the Galatians where he tells of a public confrontation with Peter. They had been in Antioch
together and Peter had taken his meals with the new
Christians converted from the gentiles. But when
some conservative Jewish Christians came from Jerusalem with James Peter did not want to offend them
and so withdrew from the gentile converts and had
his meals only with the Jewish Christians. Other
Jewish Christians did the same. Paul was outraged.
He reminded Peter that although they were both born
and bred Jews, they had come to realise that they had
not been saved by fulfilling all the Jewish legal
requirements. They had found salvation only when
they had put their faith and trust in Christ. As a
consequence of this they had abandoned the Jewish
racial taboos. If they went back on this new freedom

they were implying that the liberty Christ had given them was itself sinful. He repeats that it is only through faith in Christ that true righteousness before God is given. This is his theme in other letters too. We cannot prove that Luke had read any of the letters before he wrote his gospel some years afterwards but he must have heard Paul expounding these ideas and insisting on them many times and to many audiences. It is also plain from the whole emphasis of the gospel that he fully accepted what Paul had taught him.

Luke says that Jesus told this story to certain people who thought they were righteous and despised others. It is therefore correct to apply it to our own individual position and needs, but it must also have a much wider application to the whole Church, the body of Christ's disciples in the world. The Church has always been tempted to pride in one thing or another. In the first days there was no question of pride in any external things. In the Roman Empire Christ's followers were regarded as members of a Jewish sect and it was only when the Jews decisively repudiated the Christians and refused to have them regarded as part of their community that the Church became an illegal organisation. As it was no longer part of the Jewish community it was not one of the cults officially recognised by the Roman government. This meant that the Church had no legal standing and could not register any kind of possessions. There were no church buildings or property. Paul speaks of the ministers of the Church as having nothing, but possessing all things, penniless but owning the world.

So it has often been in the history of the Christians. In 1964 I was in my office in Kampala in Uganda and was told that two men were standing outside who claimed to be bishops and wanted to see me. I went out at once and found two very tired men standing there, dressed in soiled khaki trousers and white shirts, looking very desolate. I brought them in to my office and found that they were two bishops of the Church in the Sudan. Each of them had a story to tell of pursuit by the Sudanese army, how they had hidden in the forest and how each of them had travelled at night, sometimes escaping discovery by a matter of minutes as army patrols searched for them. One of them had been living like that for three months, eating roots and leaves and occasionally encountering groups of other Christians also in hiding who could give him something more substantial. By the end of three months he had made his way through to the Uganda border, and there very happily had met his colleague who had lived in a similar way. They got on the bus to come to see me, the nearest bishop. During the journey each had written out on a sheet of exercise paper a list of the churches in his jurisdiction, and in a series of columns had noted where the church buildings or the communion vessels or the parsonage house or the bible still existed. Almost everything the Church owned had been destroyed and each man produced his soiled paper with a few crosses to mark where possessions remained. When I asked them where their wives and children were they told me that they did not know except that they were somewhere in the hands of God and that all would be well. They said that out of the present complete loss they were sure God would bring a new thing for the Sudan. Men like that, and there will be other bishops coming to the

1988 Lambeth Conference with similar stories to tell, are typical of many Christians throughout the ages who have had nothing to boast about from a temporal point of view. Yet they also may be tempted to pride, even though they have no worldly position or material possessions to boast of. When Christians are confident that they have a true knowledge of God through Jesus Christ, as the two bishops certainly had, they may be tempted to despise those who do not possess this knowledge, even though they may be the rulers of this world. Christians have often been criticised, fairly or not, by others as people who think they are 'holier than thou'. This is a very common accusation against us in this country and sometimes we deserve to be thus condemned. The knowledge of God is not a thing about which we have any right to boast because anything we have received that is good comes from God himself and must be recognised as a gift. This is a matter for thankfulness, not for self-congratulation, because we have done nothing to deserve it.

When the Roman Empire first recognised and later, from the beginning of the fourth century, embraced the Christian religion, the reasons for human pride became precisely the reasons for Christian pride. Riches increased and with official recognition came prestige and status. Within a few years the emperors were diverting the resources of the public works department from building temples to building churches. The great basilicas of Constantinople and many other cities in the Roman Empire, and particularly in Rome, were not called basilicas, kings' buildings, for nothing. The whole nature of worship had to be modified to fit the dignity and pomp of a huge building and a great deal of the family atmosphere of worship was inevitably lost. The bishops now had a respect in the eyes of the world which was flocking into the churches. They started wearing rings on their fingers and having ceremonial staves to lean on during court ceremonies just as the better class magistrates had. Justinian even presented a very splendid suit of clothes to one of the bishops of his time. So there came occasion for pride not in spiritual achievement but in worldly success. The political rivalries between Western and Eastern Empires became reflected in jealousies between the bishops of Rome and Constantinople, and it is this political effect which has persisted to the present day. There is some hope now since the last service of the Second Vatican Council in 1965 when, during the mass in St Peter's Square, the Pope and the Ecumenical Patriarch of Constantinople solemnly embraced each other and withdrew their respective excommunication made nine hundred years before.

In England, as in most Christian states, the Church was used to forward the purposes of Government. In the seventeenth century dissenters from the Church were regarded as dissenters from the State. The Quakers, the Independents and the Roman Catholics all suffered civil disabilities because of their faith. This led to the assumption among Anglicans that normal Christianity was the same as belonging to the Church of England. Those outside it were not so much despised as disregarded. Their disabilities were taken as a matter of course. This attitude has persisted almost to our own day and is not entirely dead even now. It is

12

not so much theological differences which divide the churches and make the task of recovering visible unity extremely difficult as the social attitudes and the failure to see the other person's point of view which effectively divide us. Any scheme for the recovery of visible unity will have to deal with this attitude. When the Church has been patronised by the State there has been the danger of pride in possessions or position. After Independence in Uganda the government presented Roman Catholic and Anglican bishops with Mercedes cars and in some cases re-furnished their houses or offices with expensive furniture. It was difficult to refuse this sign of regard, even though some of the bishops had qualms about it. The bishops in the fifth century and onwards, when emperors started patronising the Church, must sometimes have had similar qualms. When bishops or other church leaders are put on a par with the government officials there is always the danger of accepting the position as of right and being separated from the mass of members of the Church, especially the very poor. It seems to be true that just as individual Christians are always in danger of trusting in the wrong things and priding themselves on their possessions or their achievements, so it is also with the Church. It is natural, but wrong, for a parish priest to feel that the size of his congregations reflects his own success as a minister of the Gospel. This may be so but it certainly may not be so and to be a successful priest, in the world's terms, may mean failure in God's sight.

One of the standard techniques of a communist society is self-criticism. Lent is a time when Christians are called to self-criticism. They have to look at themselves and the corporate life of their own church and congregation in the light of Christ's own teachings and the way he embodied those teachings in his own life. This does not mean that Lent should be a time of gloom and despair. It is much more like an occasion for diagnosis of our ills in order that we might bring them to be healed. We have to try to identify the real motives of our lives and the goals we are trying to reach. The object of this exercise is to examine ourselves to see what it is in which we trust and for which we hope. It is easy to say – our hope is in you, O Lord – whereas, in fact, it is really in other things altogether, probably not in our own righteousness but it may be in our education or our spiritual attainment and the time we give to church work or something of that sort. This is, as we saw in the story Jesus told, an irrelevance and may be a positive hindrance to finding God.

Luke finishes the story of the Pharisee and the tax man in the Temple by a summary statement that the person who exalts himself will be abased and the person who humbles himself will be exalted. As Matthew quotes this same saying in a different context it seems that the first Church recognised it as a statement of Jesus but had forgotten the situation in which he first made it. The meaning is clear. But it is also a dangerous statement. Exalting yourself is an unremarkable phenomenon. We all do it at least in our own sight, and are hurt when people do not accept our own valuation of ourselves. To humble ourselves is perhaps rather dangerous because it can create at once the same kind of spiritual pride which is condemned in the story. It is also unlikely that anyone who humbles himself will succeed in convincing anyone else that he is humble. The classic case in English literature is Uriah Heep in Dickens' *David Copperfield*, probably one of the most unpleasant characters in English fiction. C. S. Lewis observed somewhere that true humility is not to think little of oneself, it is not to think of oneself at all. It is for this reason that I started this meditation with the story of Julia Potts. She did not humble herself and certainly did not exalt herself. She appeared not to think of herself at all and that's why the few people who knew her in Portsmouth those years ago found contact with her so refreshing and stimulating.

The word humble comes from the Latin humus, the soil. To be humbled is not so much to be put down by others, or put in one's place, as to be down to earth. This phrase in ordinary English means to be a person who is talking about real things and is not influenced by fantasy and wishful thinking. It is to take things as they really are and work on that base. Surely this is what Christian humility is about. It is certainly not pretending that we are strong and self-sufficient, quite the reverse. To accept ourselves as we really are is also to make us realise our need of God's forgiveness and help, which is precisely what the tax man in the story did. Paul says that when he was weak then he was strong for he found God's strength made complete and operative in his weakness. And so it will be with us this Lent if we are willing to face ourselves and to be neither shocked nor surprised at what we find, but to accept our position in relation to God with great thankfulness that this very state of things is the basis of our hope.

Lent 1 Temptation

Jesus, full of the Holy Spirit, returned from
the Jordan, and was led by the Spirit for
forty days in the wilderness, tempted by
the devil. And he ate nothing in those
days; and when they were ended, he was
hungry. The devil said to him, 'If you are
the Son of God, command this stone to
become bread.' And Jesus answered him,
'It is written, "Man shall not live by bread
alone."' And the devil took him up, and
showed him all the kingdoms of the world
in a moment of time, and said to him, 'To
you I will give all this authority and their
glory; for it has been delivered to me, and I
give it to whom I will. If you, then, will
worship me, it shall all be yours.' And
Jesus answered him, 'It is written, "You
shall worship the Lord your God, and him
only shall you serve."' And he took him to
Jerusalem, and set him on the pinnacle of
the temple, and said to him, 'If you are the
Son, throw yourself down from here; for it
is written, "He will give his angels charge
of you, to guard you," and "On their
hands they will bear you up, lest you strike

your foot against a stone."' And Jesus
answered him, 'It is said, "You shall not
tempt the Lord your God."' And when the
devil had ended every temptation, he
departed from him until an opportune
time.

(Luke 4. 1-13 RSV)

Trivandrum is a city in South India. The temple stands
in a tank, an artificial lake. Its towers are crowned
with gilded ornaments shining in the sun. The temple
compound is large and contains many buildings for all
kinds of use. Most surprising is a Christian school for
girls. This was started more than a hundred years ago
when women missionaries of the Zenana Missionary
Society became friends of the Maharajah and the
Maharani and were asked by them to undertake the
education of the caste Hindu girls. It was surprising
that they were given buildings within the temple
compound, but they have been there ever since. The
missionaries have gone now but their successors,
Indian Christians, are still allowed to work with the
Hindu girls, and apparently have never given cause
for concern about proselytism. The worship of the
school is Christian. The hymns and prayers are in the
name of Christ and the Bible is taught.

One of the teachers in this school is Mr Joseph. He
worked there for many years as a language teacher.
He was a man of Syrian Christian stock, a member of
the ancient Christian community which has been in
Kerala from the second century, if not from the first. It
is a community which was recognised by the Mahara-
jahs and given various privileges. It counted almost

like a Hindu caste, and as a price of this acceptance observed most of the Hindu rules about caste pollution. Mr Joseph taught acceptably and his material included the Hindu classics. It is an anomaly that the education of young Hindu girls has been in the hands of convinced Christians for so long.

Mr Joseph was about fifty at the time of which I am writing. He was a very gentle man, very conscientious and always busy. When he cycled home after his day's work another task awaited him. For a long time he had acted as the church teacher or catechist of a congregation of depressed class people who inhabited a plot of land called Karali about two miles away on the sea coast. I do not know when they had first become Christian but certainly Mr Joseph has looked after them for a long time. The near ancestors of these depressed class people had been serfs, tied to their landlords' paddy fields, and very rarely able to earn cash in payment for their services. During the months when there was work available they were sufficiently but very poorly fed, with no animal protein and food hardly adequate in quantity. During the months when the fields were flooded there was no work and the people were near starvation and ran up debts with the local moneylender.

Mr Joseph took services for these people, prepared them for baptism or confirmation, and sat with them in their meetings as they discussed the affairs of their community. This was an unusual position for most Syrian Christians shared the feelings about pollution of their caste Hindu neighbours, and if a backward class man was in contact with a Syrian during their work in the fields the Syrian would not return into his

19

own house before he had bathed and changed his clothes. For Mr Joseph, therefore, to be available always as the guide and counsellor of these people was in its way quite extraordinary. He must have been tempted very often to give up the work he had so generously undertaken, I think without pay. His colleagues in the Fort School would have been surprised and perhaps scandalised if they had known the extent of his commitment, and even his fellow Syrian Christians within the ordinary church congregation of Trivandrum would not have been completely happy about it. His commitment was tested in these ways, quite apart from the strain of looking after a Christian church as well as earning his living by teaching and maintaining the life of his own family.

Certainly Mr Joseph would have had no money or resources of his own to help these poor Christians in their times of starvation. There seemed only one way in which they could be helped and that way involved the repudiation of their Christianity. The State government, in common with the Central government, had a scheme for helping the most economically deprived people, that is to say the depressed classes, with various kinds of assistance. A number of jobs were reserved in the public works department and grants were given for free education of children. In times of unusual shortage there was sometimes food assistance as well. The depressed class of people all over India who had become Christians did not benefit from any of these concessions. They were held by the government to belong to an economically superior class and therefore to need no assistance. In fact, their position was no different at all from their colleagues who had not become Christians. They were in no way at an advantage over them. If a depressed class Christian wanted to obtain the benefits offered he had to go to a government registrar and change his name from a Christian to a Hindu one. Then he would benefit. It is difficult for outsiders to appreciate the strain it must have been to go on for weeks or months in abject poverty, with debts piling up, when a simple declaration in a government office could alter one's whole position. Yet the Christians felt this was impossible to do. They could not leave their Lord.

The Christians of Karali reached a point of crisis in 1945. Somehow or other they had collected money to build themselves a permanent church. It was not a very large room but it was built of brick and had a proper timber roof thatched with palm leaves. It was so much superior to their own little huts that they were extremely proud of it and conducted all their affairs within it. There was hardly any furniture except a table and the people sat on mats on the cow-dunged floor. One Sunday while they were worshipping there was shouting outside and a large group of Hindu men and youths surrounded the building and started dismantling it. They beat the people as they ran out, and they not only destroyed the roof but broke down the walls and cut down a few palm trees growing outside. The people retreated to their huts and then had a visit from the police who said that their conduct had led to a breach of the peace and that they were forbidden to worship, even in their own houses. When the men went out to work in the week human dung was thrown into their huts and the women were molested. This went on for several months. It was a very severe test of their faith in God. At the end of the year at Christmas two of their elders came to see me and asked if I would go and celebrate Holy Communion on Christmas Day. I had kept away from Karali ever since the trouble started because I thought the sight of a white face among the Christians was likely to exacerbate their troubles and Mr Joseph had agreed with this assessment. They told me now that the strain was almost too much, and although several families which had lapsed from church membership had come back in the time of trouble to support their brethren, they were almost at the end of their endurance. I cycled down on Christmas Day and found the white sand had been swept and had no speck of dirt on it, the bushes had been draped with paper chains and red hibiscus blossoms were tied on the trees and everywhere roundabout. On the sand was a table shielded a little from view by a palm leaf mat strung between two trees. The whole community was present and we started the Communion. I at least was apprehensive that we might be interrupted suddenly either by the police or by the local Hindus. Nothing happened. At the Prayer for the Church I invited them to pray and one man thanked God that at Christmastime Jesus had come not to a proper house but to a stable. He said, 'Lord, we built you a house but it is in ruins. We thank you that you come to us even though we have no house to offer you.'

It had been a rash thing for the Christians to build their little church in that particular plot. It was the only land they had but it was situated between two Hindu temples and whenever the Christians sang or

22

made their presence felt in any way the local Hindus doubtless regarded it as an affront, if not a pollution. But they persisted. I believe eventually they were able to rebuild their church sometime after I had left the district and Mr Joseph, when I last heard some years ago, was continuing his faithful ministry among them.

The theme of this Sunday is temptation and the word is applied to the experience of Christ in the wilderness immediately after his baptism. The Greek word used does not, however, carry the meaning of temptation in the sense of seducing someone from the right path and persuading them to do something they know to be wrong. We have usually interpreted the story of Jesus in the desert as the story of the devil's attempt to seduce him from what he saw to be the way of God. In fact we should do better to regard this interpretation of the story as a side issue. What happened to Jesus was that his faith in God was being tested in many ways and Jesus came through that test without compromising his trust and obedience in God.

In the New Testament the Greek word is used with the clear meaning of test and only sometimes can carry with it the suggestion that the test was a means of weakening faith. When Paul talks about the Christians of Macedonia he paints a picture which can also be applied to the Christians of Karali. He says that they were so poor that he had no intention of asking them to assist in the Christian Aid project he had set up for the Christians in Palestine who had been badly

23

affected by persecution and by political events. However, when they heard of the project the Macedonian Christians begged him to be allowed to share in this task. 'The troubles they have been through have tried them hard, yet in all this they have been so exuberantly happy that from the depths of their poverty they have shown themselves lavishly openhanded' (2 Corinthians 8.2 NEB).

There are many passages where this word to test, the word translated temptation in the theme of this Sunday, is used. Peter says, 'This is cause for great joy, even though now you smart for a little while, if need be, under trials of many kinds. Even gold passes through the assayer's fire, and more precious than perishable gold is faith which has stood the test. These trials come so that your faith may prove itself worthy of all praise, glory, and honour when Jesus Christ is revealed' (1 Peter 1, 6-7 NEB). 'Beloved, do not be surprised at the fiery ordeal which comes upon you to prove you, as though something strange were happening to you' (1 Peter 4.12 RSV). In the first letter of Peter the references in chapters 1 and 4 use the same word we have already met. The word would have been used in New Testament Greek to talk about testing an article of equipment or a domestic animal. You test them to find out what they can do, to make sure that the animal or article you are thinking of purchasing is efficient and can do what you want.

This idea of testing a material object or an animal is then transferred to human beings and we commonly use an expression like 'time of testing' for an individual or a nation who has had to endure exceptional suffering or difficulties. 'So far you have faced no trial

24

beyond what man can bear. God keeps faith, and he will not allow you to be tested above your powers, but when the test comes he will at the same time provide a way out, by enabling you to sustain it' (1 Corinthians 10.13 NEB). 'My brothers, whenever you have to face trials of many kinds, count yourselves supremely happy, in the knowledge that such testing of your faith breeds fortitude, and if you give fortitude full play you will go on to complete a balanced character that will fall short in nothing' (James 1. 2-3 NEB).

Perhaps the difference between the two English words tempt and test lies in the motive behind them. To tempt someone is a bad thing to do. The motive seems to be to bring that person down. It is a word that can only be used of a person. You can't tempt a cow or a car. To test or prove an object, on the other hand, or a person, need not be a negative thing at all. You test a bicycle before you buy it, in order to make sure that it is reliable and fulfils your requirements. And the same thing was true in New Testament times when you bought an ox for ploughing. The purpose of testing is not to do harm to a thing but to make sure that it is what you need and capable of fulfilling that need. If the word testing is usually used, instead of the word tempting, and I have suggested that this is perfectly legitimate from the Greek text, perhaps the New Testament passages about temptation are more understandable. The International Committee for English Liturgical Texts proposed common forms for liturgical expressions which are frequently used by churches which worship in the English language. They proposed forms for the Creed, the Gloria in excelsis and above all the Lord's Prayer. For many years people have found difficulty in the clause 'lead us not into temptation' because it is impossible to believe that God would do such a thing. The Committee therefore proposed that we should say 'Do not bring us to the time of trial' or 'Do not bring us to the test'. This revision was, however, rejected for use in the Church of England by the General Synod which is why we still say 'Lead us not into temptation'. The experience of many churches during this century has made them pray 'Do not bring us to the time of trial' with deep and painful meaning, but in England we have so far not been brought into that particular situation.

We cannot reflect on Luke's story of the testing of Jesus' faith in the desert without looking back to Jesus' baptism. Luke speaks of this in a surprisingly casual way (Luke 3. 21 & 22). He says that very many people came to John and were baptised by him in the River Jordan. Among those baptised was Jesus, and after he came up from the river he was praying. At that point, Luke tells us, the heavens opened and the Holy Spirit came down upon Jesus in the form of a dove and a voice was heard, it is not clear by whom, quoting Psalm 2. v.7 'My son, my beloved son on whom my favour rests'. Then Jesus, who was about thirty years old, was filled with the Spirit and led into the wilderness. (Mark says he was driven by the Spirit.)

We cannot know about Jesus' consciousness of God as he came out of the water praying. We are ignorant of his inner thoughts and feelings. Perhaps, in our own spiritual experiences, we may have a clue to understanding them. When a person asks God to come into his life, and finds that prayer answered, there is usually a great rush of feeling, the person is overwhelmed by wonder and thankfulness, and a sense of his own unworthiness. This emotion leads to a re-ordering of life with a new sense of purpose. A parallel to this spiritual experience is falling in love with a fellow human being. We never forget completely what happened to us at the beginning of conscious discipleship, or other occasions of spiritual awareness as we have lived our lives as Jesus' disciples.

What happened to Jesus was perhaps a complete experience of which our experiences are pale reflections. He became aware he was possessed by God's Spirit. He was able to trust God completely for the unknown future, and had one desire only, which was to obey God as he showed him his way day by day. Jesus was given no blueprint or strategy, he had simply to obey and leave the issue to God. He knew God was his father who would never let him go.

This self-dedication brought insight into human motives and into the history of his people. In the testing of his faith which follows he quotes the account in Deuteronomy of the desert wandering of his people and sees to the very heart of God's message to them at that time of testing and formation. He seems to have been aware that he was recapitulating in himself the calling long ago of Israel to be God's servant.

The desert was very near at hand. It is a great tract of wild country where human beings cannot live and where animals are highly specialised for that arid environment. Jesus was entirely alone. There are no paths in the desert except perhaps the fresh tracks of one of the few animals. A man can easily be lost. The English word 'bewildered' comes from the word 'wilderness' and vividly portrays the sense of losing all direction and being confused as to the best way to go. Jesus was bewildered. If the story we are considering has any historic basis, then we have a clue to the thoughts which were in Jesus' mind. Every answer he gives to the 'temptations' comes from the scriptures themselves, from the accounts of the wanderings of the people of Israel in the desert for forty years before they came to the promised land. The way those verses are used in this story shows a grasp of the real meaning which can otherwise easily be lost in a mass of detail of purported historical description. We can believe that Jesus was meditating on the plan of God for his people in the context of that history which was so important to his race as demonstrating the guiding and protecting hand of God upon them in the days when their nation was being formed.

Towards the end of the time Jesus spent wandering in the desert we are told that three temptations came to him. He noticed how some of the round flat stones looked like bread. Perhaps in their games when they played shops, the little children used such stones to stand for flat loaves of bread, which may lie behind the Lord's comment that no father, if his son asks for a loaf, will give him a stone. However that may be, the devil suggested to him that he might relieve his hunger, of which he had become acutely aware, by turning a stone into bread. Jesus sees through this suggestion at once. If indeed he is God's son, then it is true that the power of God is at his disposal. But he knows that God's power must be directed towards God's purpose and has come to see that there is no short cut in bringing men to God. The use of God's power in this way to satisfy his own hunger would be to use it in a purely selfish way breaking the natural law. It is true that in the story of the feeding of the five thousand, Jesus out of compassion, did something like this. But perhaps the main point of that story is that God is able to satisfy the physical and spiritual needs of men and women and continually does so. God normally works through the processes of nature that we know. The stone has to wear down into dust and return to the soil before it can nourish the growing seedling which will in time produce wheat and therefore bread. There is no short cut by magic allowable. Jesus replies sharply, 'Man shall not live by bread alone', which is a quotation from Deuteronomy Chapter 8, verse 3.

Luke says that the devil, having failed in his first attempt, took Jesus to a place from which he could see all the kingdoms of the world. The devil claimed that he had power over the nations of mankind and that if Jesus would only acknowledge his worthiness and worship him, he would give him authority over all the nations and great glory in the sight of men. It is perfectly clear that Luke is describing some kind of visionary experience, one it is hard to imagine. There is no doubt, however, about the reply of Jesus. He says at once, 'God alone is worthy of worship' (Deuteronomy 6. 13). Nothing else can be put into the place of God. He is saying that no compromise on fundamentals of this kind is possible.

Then again in a vision Jesus is transported to Jerusalem and taken up into one of the towers of the temple. He can see the people milling about below in the courtyard and outside the temple walls, and the suggestion comes that he should jump off. The devil supports this suggestion by two quotations from Psalm 91 which are that God will give his angels charge over him and that the angels will bear him up so that he doesn't even dash his foot against a stone. Jesus' reply is immediate, from Deuteronomy 6.16, 'You shall not tempt the Lord your God.' He has rejected also the temptation to attract men's allegiance and wonder by a magical act. He will not use the power which is his as God's son, to take any short cuts in showing men the nature of God and God's demands upon them. Sometimes the Church has fallen for this temptation trying to bring people to Christ by forms of evangelism which seem like psychological manipulation, or by offers of material advantage.

We are told that the devil had finished the tests that Jesus faced, the temptations, and left him until a suitable time to return. He certainly did not leave Jesus for ever.

We are tested every day of our lives and show what we are and what we really believe by the way we respond to what happens to us. Some testing situations we can anticipate, many occur unexpectedly. We find ourselves suddenly in a dangerous situation or we meet someone who makes demands on us. Perhaps we expose ourselves to temptation, perhaps we see someone in great need. We are tested by such events. Every crisis in our lives, small or great, is by definition a coming into judgement. We declare what we are by the way we react or respond. Jesus did this in the desert. These occasions of testing reveal the depth of our faith in God and commitment to him. What is being tested is our maturity in Christ.

This testing is a personal experience, but it is also the corporate experience of the Church from the first days until now. For three hundred years the Church lived in danger, without material resources. Then it went through centuries of state patronage. This was a time of testing whether the Church depended in reality on God or man. In times of schism and conflict the Church was tempted to forget the law of love and try to crush its adversaries by any means available. In times of acceptance by the State the Church has been tempted to enjoy its prosperity and accept the injustices and inequalities of society as protest against them would be resented by the State. When the population accepted the teaching of the Church as having divine authority, the Church sometimes used its position to enrich itself and increase its power. In times of national apostasy from theistic belief the Church has sometimes reduced its own message in an effort to make it more acceptable so that its own status in society remained. In Russia the Church was tested by the struggle for a classless society and by the official atheism of the State. In China the Church was suspect because of its foreign missionaries from the imperialist West and ordinary Chinese Christians sometimes chose death rather than repudiate their friendship with their foreign brothers and sisters in Christ.

During the Nazi period the Church in Germany was tested by a vigorous paganism of blood and soil and by a racist policy which caused the death of six million Jews. In Holland the Church struggled to maintain the place of justice against the denial of it under Nazi rule. So at every time and in every place the Church's faith and obedience is tested. To remain faithful required strength and courage from God himself. Perhaps we ought to use more often the old Franciscan prayer: 'Lord, give your Church power to walk boldly in times of danger, and warily in times of quiet.'

Perhaps also we shall be more aware this week of the way we are tested and our faith is proved in almost every situation into which we come. This will make us more dependent on the Lord who is with us, who himself has endured every kind of testing and yet was not overcome. In the last ten years the devastation of war and the death of thousands of innocent people has severely tested the faith of many Christians in Uganda. Personal tragedy often tests the faith of Christians living in the comparative security of our own nation. The trials and tribulations of the Christians of Karali tested their faith. The constant tensions in which Mr Joseph lived and worked tested his faith. Only God can give the deep inner conviction of his love and his power that enable us to meet our tests with faith that does not fail.

Lent 2   Conflict

They brought to Jesus a man who was possessed; he was blind and dumb; and Jesus cured him, restoring both speech and sight. The bystanders were all amazed, and the word went round: 'Can this be the Son of David?' But when the Pharisees heard it they said, 'It is only by Beelzebub prince of devils that this man drives the devils out.'

He knew what was in their minds; so he said to them, 'Every kingdom divided against itself goes to ruin; and no town, no household, that is divided against itself can stand. And if it is Satan who casts out Satan, Satan is divided against himself; how then can his kingdom stand? And if it is by Beelzebub that I cast out devils, by whom do your own people drive them out? If this is your argument, they themselves will refute you. But if it is by the Spirit of God that I drive out the devils, then be sure the kingdom of God has already come upon you.

'Or again, how can anyone break into a strong man's house and make off with his goods, unless he has first tied the strong man up before ransacking the house?

'He who is not with me is against me, and he who does not gather with me scatters.

'And so I tell you this: no sin, no slander, is beyond forgiveness for men, except slander spoken against the Spirit, and that will not be forgiven. Any man who speaks a word against the Son of Man will be forgiven; but if anyone speaks against the Holy Spirit, for him there is no forgiveness, either in this age or in the age to come.'

(Matthew 12. 22-32 NEB)

Desmond Tutu, Archbishop of Capetown, is a Christian leader who makes the world's headlines because he is almost always involved in controversy. To a Christian outsider relying on published speeches and the occasional sight and sound of Desmond preaching or being interviewed before a television camera he seems to be consistently faithful to his Master. Desmond stands firm on what he believes to be the clear teaching of God's word. He believes in the equality of all men and women before God which implies that they should have equality of opportunity in education and in taking responsibility for their lives and actions as individuals and as communities. Desmond believes that God wants one nation in South Africa with no race dominating the others but all contributing their particular gifts to the good of the whole. Each race should have pride in its own culture but see its primary loyalty to the nation of South Africa. The Judiciary has a reputation for impartiality and justice but the laws it administers must be made by a truly representative legislature, not one in which 80% of the population is unrepresented. There should be no detention without trial and torture may not be used in a Christian state. Desmond condemns violence whether used by the state or against the state. He refuses to abandon hope of a Christian state where all the citizens with all their differences live and work together in peace and co-operation. A reporter asked him what he felt about being thrust into the position of a political leader and he replied, 'I am a churchman and not a political leader, but while you lock up the real legitimate leaders of my people I must remain a spokesman for them.' He is a man of no political pretensions or ambitions.

Desmond Tutu has been in a position to publicise his convictions ever since he became Dean of Johannesburg in 1975 in pastoral charge of a large congregation made up of Africans, coloured people, Asians and Europeans. He rejoiced at their readiness to worship and work together and in the many signs of the unity which the Spirit gives. Desmond spoke his mind, always in charity, always with scriptural authority for the principles he enunciated and always without compromise. This won him the confidence of many Africans. There were those who were in strong opposition to him because of his rejection of violence, of his loyalty to the idea of a single nation in which all played their part and neither majority nor minority sought to dominate the rest. Almost all the white members of his church respected and admired him, but they sometimes had to face the criticism and resentment of other whites whose political stance made them suspicious of such an attitude.

Desmond became Bishop of Lesotho for a time but did not renounce his South African citizenship. Then he was elected Bishop of Johannesburg and in 1986 Archbishop of Capetown, the head of the Anglican Church in South Africa. In 1985 he was awarded the Nobel Peace Prize and his friends overseas were glad not only because he deserved it but also because it gave him international recognition which might be of help in his dealings with his government.

Desmond has always been fair and open in his dealings with the white government and tried to reason with them and also warn them that there will be terrible consequences if the apartheid system is not changed. His Open Letter to Prime Minister Vorster in 1976 was published and he has had interviews with President Botha.

Desmond Tutu is a man with an unfailing sense of humour and when his eyes twinkle behind his thick spectacles people have to smile with him. I happened to meet him when he had been appointed to Lesotho. I told him that the previous bishop visited his diocese on horseback and asked Desmond if he could ride. He told me he could not, but would have to learn. When I saw him next, two years afterwards, I asked him how he was getting on with the riding. His eyes twinkled and he said, 'Very well indeed. The other day I was visiting a congregation on the veld and was met by their menfolk, all on horseback, bringing a horse for me. We rode together at an easy pace for a mile or two. When the church buildings came into view with the congregation standing in front of them clapping, the men all galloped. As we got near,' and here his eyes

36

were greatly enlarged behind the glasses and a tone of awe came into his voice, 'I knew that nothing in heaven or earth could save me, and as I pulled up I fell off. But,' he said, 'the Basuto are very polite people and so all the men fell off too.'

Desmond does not make wild statements and he always has reasons for what he says. He is staunch because he believes he is acting in obedience to God and he has a faith that good will eventually come out of the afflictions of the present time, a faith that lesser believers find it hard to hold. Desmond's life is a life of conflict in which he has been in prison and been threatened with death but he goes cheerfully and happily on, as concerned for the white members of his flock as for the black, and not recognising any difference between them in their calling by God and their need for God.

The blind and dumb man never forgot the day when someone led him to Jesus. Jesus healed him and he saw and spoke. The glory and the wonder of it must have been unspeakable. We sometimes see on television people who have had their sight restored after being blind for many years. They are so overwhelmed with the beauty of the world and of those they love that emotion chokes their speech. This man started a new life on the day his senses were restored. This is not, however, the point of the story as we hear it in today's Gospel. It is set in a scene of conflict.

The Gospels are full of such stories for everything Jesus said or did seemed to cause offence to the governing class among the Jews. Jesus was a scandal to them in the precise sense of that word, a stone to stumble over, a rock set in the path on which people can trip and fall. Jesus observed the ordinary requirements of the Jewish law but he did not accept that obedience to its regulations overrode moral considerations or the duty to help those in need. He had been involved in controversy, over a crippled woman whom he healed in the synagogue one Sabbath. In the present story we hear no more of the exultant man who had been healed, but we are made to feel the hatred and anger which flared up against Jesus. Jesus' opponents did not have the straightforward approach of the blind man of whom we read in John 9. That man was told by the Pharisees that his healer was a sinner. He replied that he did not know about that, he knew only one thing – he had been blind and now could see. He added rather unwisely that he thought it was well known that God did not hear the prayers of sinners, a remark which nettled the men who were questioning him.

On the occasion of which we read in today's gospel the charge against Jesus is the same. The Pharisees saw the act of Jesus from an angle entirely different from that of the man who had been healed. He was overwhelmed with wonder at what had happened and he had no doubt that Jesus was acting not in his own strength or with any human power but with the power of God. In the Gospels we often find the remark, after a healing, that the power of God had been manifest in Jesus. Certainly the man who was healed saw it in that way. The Pharisees, on the other hand, were confused and frightened as well as being blinded by their prejudice. They were confused and frightened because they could not deny that something very unusual had happened, and there were witnesses standing round them joining in the man's excitement. In these circumstances they had to be careful what they said. The very enthusiasm of the crowd made them even more anxious. They did not know where this thing would stop. Jesus had no official recognition from anyone, nor had he been trained as an official teacher. But he was doing these wonderful things and people were trusting him. The Pharisees were sure they had to stop this. They were blind because they were unwilling to question their previous assumptions and to admit that this must have been the work of God. So they blurt out the bitter accusation that Jesus has done this great thing not by the power of God but by the power of Beelzebub, by the power of the devil or evil spirits. This must have been a shocking accusation to the people who heard it, as well as to the man who was healed. It was flying in the face of the facts.

The Pharisees' accusation sounds like an unpremeditated outburst of anger because otherwise they would surely have modified a statement so patently absurd. But they were really worried. The people were wondering if Jesus could possibly be the Messiah and this idea had to be scotched at once. It was very dangerous. It would lead to a clash with the Roman authorities because it might easily arouse popular unrest or even revolt. They were jealous of the way the common people listened to Jesus when they themselves were treated with respect but seldom with affection. If they had been in a different position and not outraged by this sudden and dangerous suggestion that Jesus might be the Messiah, they might have dealt with the matter more moderately. In fact, from the rest of the Gospels it would seem that, although the Pharisees occasionally had face-to-face confrontation with Jesus on various points, they did not dare to attack him so openly. We know that at least a few listened to Jesus with appreciation and hope.

Jesus had no difficulty in showing the absurdity of the Pharisees' accusation. It was thought that sickness and disease were evil, the work of devils, bad spirits. To cast out bad spirits was the work of God, but the Pharisees said Beelzebub, the prince of the devils, had effected the blind man's cure. Jesus replied that evil cannot destroy evil without destroying itself. A household divided against itself falls apart. Jesus added another argument. He said that there were Jewish healers and exorcists and asked whether they also fell under the same condemnation. The fact that there were Jews who were practising exorcism and healing was accepted by all the people as a demonstration of God's presence in their midst and of his healing power. Surely if sickness was the work of Satan it would have been absurd for Satan to cast it out and heal. Healing was a demonstration not of the power of evil but of the power of God and of good. Jesus said that if he then by the finger of God cast out evil spirits, then surely God's kingdom was in their midst. In other words, he said that the healing was a sign of the presence of God working through him and in him.

There is an interpolation here which points out that if Satan had in fact been despoiled and his power destroyed, it was a sign that one stronger than Satan had come, that is to say God himself. He had overcome Satan. According to the story Jesus added that anyone who was not working with him, was working against him. He said the same thing using another figure of speech drawn from harvesting grain. Those who did not share with him in gathering grain were scattering and wasting it.

Jesus went on to make a statement which has been a cause of considerable worry and confusion to many Christians through the centuries. He said that those who call the Holy Spirit evil are committing a sin for which there can be no forgiveness. He said that any other sin could be forgiven, even blasphemy against himself. But if anyone recognised something to be good and yet deliberately called it bad and persisted in that lie, living a lie, then he could not be forgiven. No forgiveness is possible while we wilfully persist in sin and refuse to acknowledge the truth we see, for the simple reason that we are not ready and willing to accept it.

The words of Jesus assert that our attitudes now condition our standing in the next world. It is a solemn warning. We all say foolish things under the influence of strong anger, or when our attitude to someone has hardened into rejection of that person, but we cannot hope that our anger will be an excuse for what we have said or done. These Pharisees mistrusted Jesus and were convinced that he was a threat to all they held sacred. Their anger blinded them to the truth.

When, after Jesus' death, believers were rounded up and imprisoned, or like Stephen stoned to death, they had to become accustomed to false accusations of every kind. They were accused of cannibalism in some parts of the Roman Empire on the strength of hearsay about the Eucharist, eating the body and blood of Christ, and of being atheists because they did not worship in the heathen temples. The first Christians seemed to be saying that non-believers who saw that the life of Christians was good but called it evil, could have no forgiveness because they deliberately rejected the truth they saw. The story of Jesus' life is a story of conflict, which was the inevitable result of his teaching about God and human values, in contradiction to the accepted thinking of his people, the Jews. The teaching of Jesus not only provoked his opponents to search for a way to silence him, but also challenged the day to day assumptions of his own followers. The story of Jesus' passion is a series of confrontations with village and townspeople, with the Jewish leaders and with the Roman state.

The history of the Church from the day of Pentecost is also a story of confrontation and conflict. The Christian Gospel as Paul understood it was a new and powerful idea which challenged all kinds of accepted but unexamined human assumptions. This kind of conflict is documented in the letter to the Galatians where Peter's unwillingness to offend his fellow Christians with a Jewish background leads to a sharp exchange with Paul, who wrote: 'I opposed him to his face, because he stood condemned. For before certain men came from James, he ate with the Gentiles; but when they came he drew back and separated himself, fearing the circumcision party.' (Galatians 2. 11-12 RSV) Paul considered that Peter's attitude denied the grace of God which was the heart of the Gospel. Within the Church emphasis on truth has often had the same result. Luther rediscovered the teaching of Paul through his study of Augustine, and was led to challenge many of the assumptions commonly held by Christians in the Europe of his day. It was unfortunate, but not unusual, that the opposing sides in the argument were supported by rival political interests, and so theological difference led not only to academic argument, but to armed conflict. In the history of the Church, at many times and in many places, the spirit of Christ has been denied and rejected by Christians who have tried to settle differences of opinion or tradition by force of arms, by the physical destruction of their opponents. In doing this, they have themselves come into condemnation. For centuries Moslems spoke of the Crusades as proof that Christians, with their talk of forgiveness and love, were hypocrites and liars. In our time it is reported that Moslems in the East Indies speak in a similar way of the sectarian killings in Northern Ireland, and the mutual alienation there of the Christian communities as proof of the same thing. For that matter, many secularised people in Great Britain dismiss the credibility of Christians for similar reasons. In Chapter 2 I gave examples of the ways in which the faith of Christians has been tested by the events of the present century. The same examples are also instances of the conflict which is apparently endemic to Christianity.

It seems that sometimes we are involved in conflict just because of what we are. Jesus in the Gospels did not stir up conflict deliberately. In this case it was the

speculation of the bystanders about Jesus which provoked the explosion of anger from the Pharisees.
Jesus' teaching and healing were, in the first instance,
a challenge to decision about him, whether he was the
Messiah or not. They were seen by the Pharisees as a
threat and a provocation. When the Church has been
established in an alien environment and its members
recruited from that environment and reborn as new
men and women by faith and baptism, their relatives
and former friends often turn against them. We need
not look back as far as Paul to see this happening. The
Baganda tribe in Uganda had been ruled by a god
king, the Kabaka, who had absolute power over his
subjects. When the first Christian converts were baptised they recognised the supreme authority of God,
which was treason in the eyes of the rulers. The first
believers were burned alive, but they died praising
God from the flames, and the Church of today was
born in these fires. An Indian Moslem shopkeeper in
Uganda was comforted by the local Anglican priest
when his wife died. He came to believe in Christ and
asked for baptism. The result was that his children
were taken from him and his house and shop destroyed, and he was excommunicated by his former
community. He found new comfort and support only
from his fellow believers of another race. In such
instances the Christians do not seek conflict, but it
sometimes comes to them willy nilly. One man's
decision for Christ often leads to many others
rejecting his claim out of fear that their old identity as
a community will be destroyed.

There are other occasions in which Christians seem
to ask for trouble by the way they confront others with

their claims. The conflict between Peter and Paul at Antioch over Jewish taboos is an example of this. Many of the dissidents in the Soviet Union have a religious basis for their protests and consequent conflict with the state. The state does not punish religious beliefs as such, but rejects teaching which it regards as inspired by the philosophy of individuality which informs Western capitalist culture and is in opposition to the community based morality of Communism. Some of the conflicts in which we find ourselves involved because we are Christians are the result of our rejection of some elements in our secular culture. Culture, and the religion which is a part of it, is the bond which holds a community together and establishes the identity of those who belong to it. Any who convert from their inherited culture and religion to a different faith are seen as potential, if not actual, traitors, and must be deprived of their rights as citizens so that they cannot spread the infection of their ideas and weaken the bonds of their community. It does not usually carry conviction if the Christians tell their native community that they are still loyal to it and pray for it, although they now belong to a body with no national boundaries, and say that their citizenship is in heaven. Tertullian remarked in the third century that there were so many Christians in the world that they could have been a serious menace to the Empire, had they been so minded. He said that they were, in fact, most loyal servants of the emperor and prayed for him and for the state, though not in the temples dedicated to his worship.

Whenever Christians express views about social evils like racism or bad housing in the inner city or nuclear disarmament, they are accused by some politicians of meddling in politics and told to return to the preaching of the Gospel. These Christians cannot in conscience keep silent if they believe that their convictions are the consequence of their faith, even though other Christians may not agree with their conclusions. In this case it may be agreed that the conflict is of our making, but we may have to say with Luther, 'Here I stand, I can do no other'. All Christians ought to try to understand their motives, if they find themselves in conflict with others. If we do not get involved in conflict at all, perhaps we should ask how committed we are to our faith in Christ and its consequences in life.

There is yet another area of conflict which Christians experience within themselves. The classic expression of this is found in Paul's letter to the Romans. 'I discover this principle, then; that when I want to do the right, only the wrong is within my reach. In my inmost self I delight in the law of God, but I perceive that there is in my bodily members a different law, fighting against the law that my reason approves, and making me a prisoner under the law that is in my members, the law of sin. Miserable creature that I am, who is there to rescue me out of this body doomed to death? God alone, through Jesus Christ our Lord! Thanks be to God!' (Romans 7. 21-25 NEB). The only resolution of this conflict is the mastering of our lower nature, the flesh Paul calls it, by the Spirit. We are told by John that love in its fullness casts out fear. It casts out many other self-centred feelings as well. Paul tells us that this love is poured into our hearts by the Holy Spirit God gives us

(Romans 5.5). It is our desire to be controlled in our whole being by the Spirit which enables God freely to work in us. The desire must be there. St Catherine of Sienna said that God does not ask a perfect work but infinite desire. Perhaps our prayer for Lent should be that of Richard of Chichester: 'Lord, may I know you more clearly, love you more dearly and follow you more nearly day by day.' Then in his Spirit we shall neither seek conflict nor evade it, but endure it in the hope and confidence that God is in it with us and our endurance is for his kingdom. He might not express it in this particular way, but it seems to be the hope and prayer of Archbishop Desmond Tutu as he goes steadily and courageously through all the conflicts which surround him.

Lent 3   Suffering

When Jesus came to the region of Caesarea Philippi he put this question to his disciples, 'Who do people say the Son of Man is?' And they said, 'Some say he is John the Baptist, some Elijah, and others Jeremiah or one of the prophets.' 'But you,' he said, 'who do you say I am?' Then Simon Peter spoke up, 'You are the Christ,' he said, 'the Son of the living God.' Jesus replied, 'Simon son of Jonah, you are a happy man! Because it was not flesh and blood that revealed this to you but my Father in heaven. So I now say to you: You are Peter and on this rock will I build my Church. And the gates of the underworld can never hold out against it. I will give you the keys of the kingdom of heaven: whatever you bind on earth shall be considered bound in heaven; whatever you loose on earth shall be considered loosed in heaven.' Then he gave the disciples strict orders not to tell anyone that he was the Christ.

From that time Jesus began to make it clear to his disciples that he was destined to go to Jerusalem and suffer grievously at the hands of the elders and chief priests and scribes, to be put to death and to be raised up on the third day. Then, taking him aside, Peter started to remonstrate with him, 'Heaven preserve you, Lord,' he said, 'this must not happen to you.' But he turned and said to Peter, 'Get behind me, Satan! You are an obstacle in my path, because the way you think is not God's way but man's.'

Then Jesus said to his disciples, 'If anyone wants to be a follower of mine, let him renounce himself and take up his cross and follow me. For anyone who wants to save his life will lose it; but anyone who loses his life for my sake will find it. What, then, will a man gain if he wins the whole world and ruins his life? Or what has a man to offer in exchange for his life?

'For the Son of Man is going to come in the glory of his Father with his angels, and when he does, he will reward each one according to his behaviour. I tell you solemnly, there are some of these standing here who will not taste death before they see the Son of Man coming with his Kingdom.'

(Matthew 16. 13-end JB)

Mother Teresa of Calcutta is one of the best known Christians in the world, yet she has always shunned publicity. The fact that her name is so well known is not a sign of success in a worldly sense, but seems to show that the world recognises love when it sees it. Mother Teresa is a short frail woman of Albanian stock who dresses in the cheap cotton sari that a poor village woman in India would wear. She's not beautiful in features but when she smiles, which she often does, the whole world around her lights up. She grew up in a very happy home in Skopje in Yugoslavia, and was called to the religious life during her school days. She did not want to leave her home and parents but she obeyed. 'She accepted ecclesiastical authority in the same unquestioning way that peasants accept the weather or sailors storms at sea. It would never occur to her either to venerate or to challenge it. So she just waited patiently' (Malcolm Muggeridge, *Something Beautiful for God*, p. 19). She was admitted to the Loreto Sisters and eventually was posted to one of their schools in Calcutta. Here Sister Teresa taught and loved the middle class girls who were educated within the protecting walls of the school. One day she had occasion to go into a basti, a slum area of temporary shelters with many people crowded together in destitution, with no proper services like water or sanitation, and with little hope of anything better. Sister Teresa was appalled and could not forget what she had seen. Eventually, on a train journey to the hills for a summer break, she received a second vocation, to serve the poor. She insists she had no vision but only a sudden inner and complete certainty that this was the will of God. Her new vocation meant that she must be released from her order by her local bishop, and then make a new rule for a new community which had to be authorised by the Pope. Her bishop and Rome between them delayed this for nearly eighteen months, but at last she was free to leave and went to a house in Calcutta. She called her new order the Missionaries of Charity. She went into the bastis and collected some children to form a little school there. From then on Mother Teresa's life has been one of constant, consistent waiting on God, to see what he would do next. I heard her tell of the early days. She was out with one of her sisters, when they heard a feeble cry from a dustbin. They looked inside and found bundled up the just living body of an old man who had been rejected as trash and left to die. For Mother Teresa no human being could ever be trash. The man was pulled out and carried home, to be bathed and cared for, and helped to die with dignity and a measure of comfort.

Mother Teresa was soon joined in her life of hardship and service by young women and men. There are now over 1500 sisters and brothers in the Missionaries of Charity, not only in Indian cities but throughout the world. In 1986 we read in the English papers of a tragedy in Tanzania. Mother Teresa had been flown in a light plane to visit three of her sisters. When the plane left it swerved from the runway and several people, including two of the sisters she had just visited, were killed. Mother Teresa lamented that they would not be dead if she had not wanted to see them.

From the time that Mother Teresa left the security of the Loreto School until the present time she has lived with suffering. This has not been only the harsh discipline of living like the poor, which all members of her order accept, but the pain of living amidst human sorrow and deprivation and realising their service is inadequate, and is in any case hardly scratching the surface of an enormous problem. Of course, when a large community of young women is living together, there are occasions of hilarity, even in the midst of the general squalor and sadness which surround them. In the early days of her work Mother Teresa and one or two sisters would travel round Calcutta in a very ancient cart, drawn by a rather decrepit but faithful old horse. They visited people and collected the sick to take them back for treatment and care. The day came when the poor old horse died. The sisters prayed that the Lord would supply them with another horse. They had no money to buy one, and it seemed quite essential to their work. The following morning they came out from chapel and saw in the compound a most splendid horse standing there. So they harnessed him to the cart and drove off, full of thankfulness. The horse, which was very strong and beautiful, proved an excellent carthorse. They used him for two days. On the second evening when they drove back, they found a prosperous Indian gentleman in their compound. He looked absolutely aghast when he saw them, and asked them if they knew what the horse was. They said they did not, and he then told them that this was the most valuable racehorse in India which had escaped from his stables down the road two days before. They told him that the horse was also good at pulling carts. The racehorse owner took his valuable animal away but I understand that he did send another horse to replace him.

Mother Teresa must be a little confused by the way her work has grown and is supported by businesslike organisations of friends all over the world. It seems that she is truly humble and, like Julia Potts, does not think of herself at all. She has only one reply when asked why she does her work. 'Christ is in them and when I serve them I am serving him.' It is axiomatic for her that the person who loves God must love his brother also. Such loving inevitably involves suffering, but Mother Teresa does not speak of that.

The Scripture passages chosen as the Gospel this Sunday contain verses which are, at first sight, difficult to accept, and may not seem to fit our understanding of Christ and his task. The disciples had the same difficulty. They also did not understand what Jesus was saying. For us the problem is greater. We do not know how far we have the actual words of Jesus and how far the editorial handling of the writer may have altered the original setting and sequence of Jesus' words. If you compare different English versions you will see that the same Greek word is translated by different English words, and this sometimes obscures rather than clarifies the meaning.

In the Gospel which has been chosen to illustrate this Sunday's theme of suffering Matthew first establishes who this Jesus is who is to suffer. In Caesarea Philippi, some miles north of the Sea of Galilee, he asks his disciples about popular gossip. What are people saying about him? Who do they think he is? The answer was that there was a good deal of speculation about him. The people identified him as one of the old prophets risen from the dead, or even as John the Baptist, whom Herod had killed not long before, brought back to life. He asked them what they themselves believed and Peter, apparently speaking for

53

them all, said that they believed he was the Messiah, the servant of God who had come in the power of God to deliver his people. The expression 'Son of the living God', which Matthew adds to Mark's account on which the story we have here is based, may not have meant then what we would mean by such words now, i.e. that Jesus shared the divine nature. Probably it meant that he shared the nature of God in the same way that any righteous man was understood to share God's nature. The righteous man showed by his life who his father really was. The phrase is used in some of the Psalms which the first Christians often quoted, as in Psalm 2 at the baptism. Jesus did not answer to the common expectations of how the Messiah would behave when he came, but nevertheless the disciples, his daily companions, were certain in their minds that no other description was adequate. They could only affirm their conviction. They could not defend it by showing how their master fulfilled the popular hope because he did not. Jesus accepted that affirmation as sufficient. He told Peter that he was not just repeating a human assessment but was responding to God's word to him. Because he had listened to God and responded to God he would rightly be called Peter, or Cephas in Aramaic, the rock man.

This statement of Jesus has been the subject of controversy down the centuries. It seems to mean that God's people, the Church, will be built not on any single human being, not even Peter, and his successors, nor on the statement Peter has just made on faith in Jesus as the Messiah, but on Peter as long as he is the man living in trust and dependence on Jesus. Augustine said, 'We Christians believe not in Peter, but in him in whom Peter believed' (*City of God* 18.54 cit. H. Chadwick, *Augustine* p.83). Paul said that he lived by faith in the Son of God who loved him and gave himself for him. So Peter, while he trusts and confesses to that faith, becomes a man on whom the Church can be built. When Peter, filled with the Holy Spirit and the courage which the Spirit gave, proclaimed Jesus on the day of Pentecost, three thousand people believed and were added to the Church.

The Lord's promise to them that the gates of the underworld can never hold out against the Church is an illustration of the problem of communication. It seems that the underworld is thought of as the sphere of death or the Devil trying to enclose all human beings within its gates and make them its captives. Perhaps the translation, the powers of hell, is slightly more understandable. All these expressions are trying to give a mental picture of what we cannot imagine, let alone understand with our reason. The Church is saying that Christ's kingdom will not be overthrown by evil, whether in Nero's persecution of A.D. 64, or at any other time in history. It is a declaration of faith. When we consider this promise many centuries later its truth is not obvious. The strong churches in North Africa, for example, and many in Asia Minor were no longer operating, except in Egypt, after the Moslem invasion of the 7th century. Perhaps even before that event they were weakened by divisions and had lost the faith which Jesus praised in Peter. We cannot know the reason for their decline and fall. On the other hand, in spite of all the sins and apostasy of the Church from the way of Christ it has persisted, and has had springtimes of renewal, especially in Europe, until the present day. To some, looking at the checkered history of the Church, its very persistence in spite of its failures seems a proof of the existence of God.

Matthew tells us that Jesus then elaborated his promise in a way not recorded by Mark or Luke, when he said he would give Peter the keys of the kingdom of heaven. This has been interpreted in the tradition of the Roman Catholic Church as a privilege belonging solely to Peter as the first Bishop of Rome, and to his successors. This divine authority bestowed special powers on them, not only to absolve or retain sins, but to have the final word in all kinds of disputes within the Church. Christians of other traditions have not been able to accept this claim in its entirety, but certainly the whole Church believes that it is responsible for proclaiming and mediating God's forgiveness of all who repent. One way in which this forgiveness is withheld is to excommunicate sinners, excluding them from the forgiven community and restoring them with joy to its common life when they repent. This practice has fallen out of use in the Church of England but it is still found in the younger churches. When a penitent comes to a priest to confess sins to God in his presence, it is, in any case, clear that the priest, in pronouncing absolution, is doing so as a servant and spokesman of the whole body, not in some private capacity.

This episode centred on Peter may seem an intrusion into the movement of the story. Jesus' command to his disciples to tell no one who he is, presumably because their idea of the Messiah and his work was so far removed from the reality, could well follow directly on Peter's confession. Jesus then goes on to the statement which is the reason this passage is read on the Sunday when we are considering Christ's suffering and our suffering. 'From that time Jesus began to make it clear to his disciples that he was destined to go to Jerusalem and suffer grievously at the hands of the elders and chief priests and scribes, to be put to death and to be raised up on the third day.' After this central statement there follow other sayings and incidents which derive from the prediction of suffering.

Peter was very shocked by Jesus' words. He took Jesus away from the others and remonstrated with him. For him, it was unthinkable that the Messiah should suffer, and he was now sure that Jesus was the Messiah. Jesus had just praised Peter for listening to God. Now he called Peter Satan because he was thinking like his contemporaries about the Messiah. He was not hearing what God was saying. Certainly at the moment no Church could be built on him. According to this account in Matthew, Jesus then told the disciples that as the Messiah would have to suffer and die, so also his disciples must be prepared for a similar fate. They must be willing to give up any selfish motives in following him, they must be willing to accept rejection and disgrace, as happened to a man condemned by the Roman Government, who had to carry his cross to the place of execution. Jesus said that the person who would give up his psyche for his sake would find a renewed and matured self. Self-centredness and self-concern would mean destruction. In popular English the Greek word 'psyche' is now used and understood. It need not be translated

57

by life or soul, or with the New English Bible safety or self. The being of a human person, the psyche, is the most precious thing there is, and nothing can be compared with it in value or importance.

In the time of Jesus many books were in circulation describing the events at the end of time. These books are called revelations or apocalypses. In the New Testament we have the Revelation of St John, and in the first three Gospels there are passages written in this highly pictorial, imaginative style. At the end of this grim passage about the suffering of the Messiah and the need for his followers to be prepared to share in such suffering, Matthew gives an apocalyptic saying. The purpose of inserting it here is probably to comfort the readers of the Gospel. Jesus spoke, according to Matthew, of his coming again in glory with the angels, to reward those who have followed him faithfully. In this passage he says nothing about the punishment of those who have been false. He adds that some of those with him at the time would not die. We are reminded of a reference to this in John 21.21, when Peter inquires about the destiny of another disciple after having been warned of his own death. There have always been those in the Church who have taken these apocalyptic sayings literally, but there have also been others who understand the glory that shall be revealed as having been revealed in the limitless self-giving of God shown once and for all and for ever in the cross of Christ.

In the Authorised Version, the word suffering is common and is used to translate a number of Hebrew and Greek words. Two Greek verbs convey the modern English usage of suffering as the experience

58

of pain, physical or mental, which can have a variety of causes. The root meaning of the word in the New Testament is, however, different. It means to allow something to happen, to bear or endure what comes to you, to put up with unpleasant events. Jesus says, 'Suffer the little children to come to me', which means 'Allow them to come to me'. This is the meaning of the Greek word most commonly used. In his book, *The Stature of Waiting*, W. H. Vanstone applies this understanding of suffering to the Passion of Christ. *Passio* is a Latin word derived from the Greek which also means bearing something, enduring it. Christ's Passion is precisely his acceptance of what happened to him. Vanstone points out that in the first part of Mark's Gospel until the moment that Judas Iscariot hands him over to his enemies, Jesus is the subject of almost every sentence. It is he who speaks, heals, commands, initiates and carries out actions. From the moment that Jesus is handed over he is no longer active, but passive. He is now the object of verbs rather than the subject. He is taken to the High Priest, transferred to Herod, brought back again, brought to Pilate, bound, scourged, crucified. He suffered many things at the hands of the elders and priests. He did not resist. He let it all happen to him. Yet in that suffering, in his passive role to which such a large section of all four Gospels is devoted, he won the salvation of mankind. By his passion and precious blood he redeemed the world, the Church has always believed. Paul, in Romans 8, says that if we suffer with Christ we shall also reign with him, share his glory. He uses a word for suffering derived for the same root as the word Peter uses in the following passage from his epistle, which I print in full because it expresses perfectly the New Testament attitude to our suffering as we try to follow Christ.

> For it is a fine thing if a man endure the pain of undeserved suffering because God is in his thoughts. What credit is there in fortitude when you have done wrong and are beaten for it? But when you have behaved well and suffer for it, your fortitude is a fine thing in the sight of God. To that you were called, because Christ suffered on your behalf, and thereby left you an example; it is for you to follow in his steps. He committed no sin, he was convicted of no falsehood; when he was abused he did not retort with abuse, when he suffered he uttered no threats, but committed his cause to the One who judges justly. In his own person he carried our sins to the gibbet, so that we might cease to live for sin and begin to live for righteousness. By his wounds you have been healed. You were straying like sheep, but now you have turned towards the Shepherd and Guardian of your souls.
>
> (1 Peter 2. 19-end. NEB)

In this passage are direct quotations from the song of the suffering servant in Isaiah 53. We read there that people marvelled at the servant of God. His suffering seemed undeserved and pointless but he accepted what came. He absorbed into himself the hatred and cruelty of his enemies. It did not express itself in reciprocal hatred, it was stopped and its power cancelled out. No one knows about whom this song was written, whether the servant of God was his people Israel, or an individual, or the Messiah to come. Certainly here the song spoke to Peter of Jesus and Jesus alone. The song is a song of hope. The servant, by bearing all evil, takes it away and sets his people free. He trusts only in God and by his letting things happen to him without ever breaking his confidence in God's love, he brings new hope to the world. This is the basis of Christian hope. The way of victory glimpsed by Isaiah was actually trodden by Jesus as far as Calvary. This had become for Christians the place of victory. There his self-giving, his sacrifice was complete. He had loved his own to the end. The tree of shame had become the tree of glory.

Christians are involved in the pain and anxiety which is never far from human life. Some suffering may be caused by factors for which humans seem to have no responsibility, cholera epidemics or earthquakes or typhoons. Some suffering may be the result of natural causes for which, however, man must accept some responsibility, diseases like AIDS, many famines, war. Although the media bring to our notice all kinds of calamities which befall our fellow human beings in many parts of the world, our emotional response is sometimes deadened because our imaginations cannot stand any more horror. We all know how we eventually disregard pictures of starving children which called out for sympathy and practical help when we first saw them. If we have some personal link with the sufferers, then love is involved, and we shall suffer with them and try to help. Many people give their services through the relief agencies and share other people's suffering. Sometimes Mother Teresa's work has been criticised because she can do so little for so great a need, and every relief worker feels that, as do social workers in our country. But we nevertheless do what we can, little though it may be, because we believe that suffering on behalf of or with others is somehow worthwhile and constructive. Christians hold on to this because of their faith in a crucified and risen Lord. Perhaps this is the chief lesson of this Sunday. It is that action springing from love, which Paul describes as taking the other person's interests as seriously as you take your own (Philippians 2.4 NEB), that is never wasted, though it may have no quick results or any perceptible results at all.

The other dimension of this suffering is that which involves us corporately as a Christian community. In this century many churches have suffered persecution and loss, and some have come out of their ordeals cleansed and revived. It was thought that the Church in China, suppressed by the Communist revolution had virtually disappeared. Only a few Christians were known to be continuing in their faith. But as soon as a more liberal regime took power a few years ago the churches sprang up like mushrooms from the earth, and in 1986 a new church building was opened in China every day of the year. Other examples are the Churches in Russia and the Eastern bloc countries, and most recently in Ethiopia. In these countries the persecution of the Church happened because power was taken by Communist regimes, explicitly atheistic in their ideology. The materialist society of the West, even though not denying God, may well be a more dangerous enemy of true Christianity than a system openly opposed to it, because there are seductive pressures to conform to a view of man and his goals which presuppose material wellbeing as the supreme good and profitability as the measure of human success. Christ tells us that we cannot be at the same time slaves of God and mammon. When the Church takes a different stance from those in authority on social matters or race relations it has to bear the consequences of its opposition.

The effects of suffering seem conditioned by our attitude towards it. If we try to bear our sufferings cheerfully without rancour or recrimination, praying for those who despitefully use us and concerned for them because the damage they are doing to themselves may be worse than that they are inflicting on others, then our suffering may be a positive thing, cleansing and constructive. If we respond with hatred and self pity, then we are destroyed by our suffering. Peter pointed this out in the first century. Desmond Tutu points it out in our own time. If a Church is weak, without political influence, as was the case of the early Church in the Roman Empire, the Uganda Church in the 1880s, the mass movement churches in the Tamil and Telugu areas of South India in the mid-nineteenth century, or the Amerindian churches in Central America, there is no other action possible than to endure the suffering, to allow their enemies to do as they please. The Lord did not call on legions of angels to rescue him.

If the Church has political power it is hard for it to be faithful to Christ's way. It may be felt that it would be quite wrong to allow, to suffer enemies of the Church to do what they want, and that all the Church's resources and influence must be used for its preservation. Tertullian pointed out, as we have seen, that the early Church did not take that line, though it would have been possible.

This business of suffering, of letting things happen to you, raises acute problems for the Church and for individual Christians. Are we to be quietist and wait for things to happen to us without influencing events? Some Christians have seen a possible alternative in the Satyagraha teaching of Gandhiji in India. In 1939 I was travelling in a train from Madras to Travencore. In my compartment were six men dressed in khaddar, the home-woven cotton cloth which was the badge of the Congress movement. They had come to offer non-violent resistance in Travancore State against what they believed to be the tyranny of the then state government. As we drew into the first railway station within the state territory we saw a strong force of police armed with iron tipped long staves waiting for them in the station yard, for they had given notice of their arrival. The youngest among them cringed at the sight but the others formed up round him, protecting him, and they marched out of the station giving up their tickets, and then folding their arms so that they should not be tempted to hit back. They stepped outside and were felled to the ground under a hail of savage blows. As the train moved on and the scene passed from sight, I felt ashamed and exalted. I was ashamed at the brutality of the police and exalted by the deliberate acceptance of such pain. These men clearly thought that their cause was worth such suffering.

In daily life we are often in the same quandary. What is the Christian thing to do? To suffer evil or to oppose it? This Sunday helps us to reflect on this problem. The problem is so difficult it is no wonder that pacifism has been a burning issue among Christians this century, in time of war and in connection with nuclear weapons. It is very difficult to apply Christ's example to such immense problems, which we confront in such intensity in our own times. Mother Teresa is clearly following in the way of acceptance of whatever comes to her in the steps of her master, Christ. Each of us has to consider what our own response should be.

Lent 4　The Transfiguration

Jesus took Peter, James, and John the brother of James, and led them up a high mountain where they were alone; and in their presence he was transfigured; his face shone like the sun, and his clothes became white as light. And they saw Moses and Elijah appear, conversing with him. Then Peter spoke: 'Lord', he said, 'how good it is that we are here! If you wish it, I will make three shelters here, one for you, one for Moses and one for Elijah.' While he was still speaking, a bright cloud suddenly overshadowed them, and a voice called from the cloud: 'This is my Son, my Beloved, on whom my favour rests; listen to him.' At the sound of the voice the disciples fell on their faces in terror. Jesus then came up to them, touched them, and said, 'Stand up; do not be afraid.' And when they raised their eyes they saw no one, but only Jesus.

On their way down from the mountain, Jesus enjoined them not to tell anyone of the vision until the Son of Man had been raised from the dead. The disciples put a question to him: 'Why then do our teachers say that Elijah must come first?' He replied, 'Yes, Elijah will come and set everything right. But I tell you that Elijah has already come, and they failed to recognise him, and worked their will upon him; and in the same way the Son of Man is to suffer at their hands.' Then the disciples understood that he meant John the Baptist.

(Matthew 17. 1-13 NEB)

Bishop Festo Kivengere tells the following story which I am allowed to reproduce in his own words.

In 1973 President Amin of Uganda announced over the radio that a number of men had been arrested for subversive activities. The military tribunal had decided to hold public executions in different parts of the country, each man to be shot in his home community as a warning to others. Three of these were men of my diocese whose families I knew well. . . .

February 10 began as a sad day for us in Kabale. People were commanded to come to the stadium and witness the execution by a firing squad of the three young men of our area. Death permeated the atmosphere in that stadium. A silent crowd of about three thousand was there to watch the spectacle.

I had permission from the authorities to speak to the men before they died, and two of my fellow ministers were with me.

They brought the men in a truck and unloaded them. They were handcuffed and their feet were chained. The firing squad stood at attention. As we walked into the centre of the stadium, I was wondering what to say to these men in the few minutes we had before their death. How do you give the Gospel to doomed men who are probably seething with rage?

We approached them from behind, and as they turned around to look at us, what a sight! Their faces were all alight with an unmistakable glow and radiance. Before we could say anything, one of them burst out:

'Bishop, thank you for coming! I wanted to tell you. The day I was arrested, in my prison cell, I asked the Lord Jesus to come into my heart. He came in and forgave me all my sins! Heaven is now open, and there is nothing between me and my God! Please tell my wife and children that I am going to be with Jesus. Ask them to accept Him into their lives as I did.'

The second man told us a similar story, excitedly raising his hands, which rattled his handcuffs. Then the youngest said:

'I once knew the Lord, but I went away from Him and got into political confusion. After I was arrested, I came back to the Lord. He has forgiven me and filled me with peace. Please tell my parents (they are evangelists in the diocese) and warn my younger brothers never to go away from the Lord Jesus.'

I felt that what I needed to do was to talk to the soldiers, not to the condemned. So I translated what the men had said into a language the soldiers understood. The military men were standing there with their guns cocked, and bewilderment on their faces. Those in the stadium who were near enough could hear it too, and the rest could see the radiance on the faces of the condemned which showed they were forgiven souls.

The soldiers were so dumbfounded at the faces and words of the men they were about to execute that they even forgot to put hoods over their faces!

The three faced the firing squad standing close together. They looked toward the people and began to wave, handcuffs and all. The people waved back. Then shots were fired, and the three were with Jesus.

We stood in front of them, our own hearts throbbing with joy, mingled with tears. It was a day never to be forgotten. Though dead, the men spoke loudly to all of Kigezi District and beyond, so that there was an upsurge of life in Christ, which challenges death and defeats it . . . .

We heard that the soldiers who were in the firing squad and the guards standing by could not shake off the reality of what they saw – the glory of God on the faces of dying men.

In the 1662 Book of Common Prayer, 6 August is the date on which the Transfiguration of Christ is to be celebrated, but until 1927 no provision was made for a collect or proper readings. 6 August is the day on which the Eastern Church also remembers this event. In the Alternative Service Book of 1980, however, the Transfiguration is to be observed on the fourth Sunday in Lent, the day the event has been remembered in the Roman Catholic Church. This change is plainly right. In the Gospel story there is a sequence of events in the life of Jesus. According to the first three Gospels, Jesus' ministry started with his baptism. Then came the testing in the desert, the confession of Peter at Caesarea Philippi and Jesus' prediction of his suffering and his statement of the conditions of discipleship. There follows at once in all three Gospels the story of the Transfiguration. This sequence of events in the Gospels is also the sequence of our meditation in the weeks of Lent.

Matthew gives a curiously stark account of the Transfiguration of Christ. He tells us simply that Jesus took Peter, James and John up into a high mountain. We gather from Luke that this happened one evening, because Jesus wanted to get away from other people to pray. He seems to have prayed all night. The three disciples, as in Gethsemane, fell asleep through exhaustion. They woke to the sound of voices, and, as they opened their eyes, were astounded and frightened by what they saw. Matthew gives none of these details. He says that the disciples saw Jesus' face shining like the sun, and his clothes also shining as white as the light, with a whiteness no human cleansing could achieve. Two men were talking with Jesus. The disciples recognised them as Moses and Elijah. Peter said the first thing that came into his head. He blurted out that it was good for them to be there, and offered to build three shelters, like the booths constructed at the Feast of Tabernacles, for Jesus and his two guests. Then a bright cloud came down on the mountain and they heard a voice, which terrified them, so that they prostrated themselves on the ground, not daring to look any more, nor wanting to hear any more. Jesus came and reassured them by the touch of his hand. He told them not to be afraid. When they had summoned courage to open their eyes again, they saw Jesus, looking as he always did, alone, with no-one else. Even though Luke says the disciples kept awake, the whole story reads like a dream, but it was shared by the three disciples, Jesus' closest friends, and afterwards became part of the preaching, proving that Jesus was indeed the Christ, the Son of the living God, as Peter had once said at Caesarea.

In the story it appears that the disciples at once recognised the two who were talking with their master. We are not told how they did so. Moses and Elijah were founders of the Jewish faith. Moses had given them the Law, the instructions about the way of life acceptable to God which the Jews received when the covenent with God was made. Jesus was speaking with this great hero, apparently not as an equal but as a superior, indeed as God. In the Old Testament story

God's radiance had been reflected on the face of Moses. Now he stood in the radiance of Christ. Elijah, the great prophet who had fearlessly spoken to kings and rulers in the name of God, and had been taken up into heaven at the end of his earthly service, was also there, in the same position as Moses in relation to Jesus. In the vision granted to the disciples Jesus was shown to fulfil the Law and the Prophets.

The voice that came from the cloud repeated the words which had been heard at Jesus' baptism, according to Luke's account. 'Thou art my beloved Son; with thee I am well pleased' (Luke 3.22 R.S.V). These words are a quotation from Psalm 2.7, where they are spoken of the king of Israel, of David's family. They picture God presenting the anointed king to the people, just as the king or queen of England, after anointing and crowning, is presented to the people as their lawful sovereign. At his baptism and his transfiguration, these same words are used of Jesus. He too has been anointed by God, not with oil but with the Holy Spirit. He is thus the true anointed one, the Messiah or, in Greek, the Christ. It is suggested that the words Matthew adds are taken from the Servant Song in Isaiah 42.1, but this is disputed. If it is so, then here may be a clue to the early Church's understanding of Jesus as the Servant of God, who suffers for his people, but will triumph in the end because God is with him. It is, however, only in 1 Peter that the references to the suffering servant of Isaiah 53 are explicit. The conversation between the risen Jesus and his two disciples, on the road to Emmaus, seems to support the view that the first disciples came to understand the suffering of Jesus in some such way. ' "How dull you are. . . . How slow to believe all that the prophets said! Was the Messiah not bound to suffer thus before entering upon his glory!" Then he began with Moses and all the prophets, and explained to them the passages which referred to himself in every part of the scriptures.' (Luke 24. 25-27 NEB.)

Today's Gospel tells how the disciples returned to the plain and to the realities of ordinary life after the wonderful happenings on the mountain. Jesus said they must keep their experience to themselves. We are not told how the disciples replied to this admonition. They were puzzled about the popular belief that God would send Elijah to prepare the nation to receive their Messiah when it was time for him to come, and they questioned Jesus about this. He said that this idea was correct, and that God had already sent his prophet in the person of John the Baptist. He added that the people had not understood, and so John had been killed. He said that this would happen to him also. He may have used the expression 'Son of Man' to refer to himself as a synonym for 'I', the first person singular pronoun, or even for 'this man'. He may have used the phrase as a reference to the coming Messiah. We do not know. The idea that the Messiah would have to suffer was, as we have already seen, unacceptable and offensive to the Jews. The presence of Moses and Elijah in the vision made clear to the disciples that Jesus had fulfilled the Law given by Moses. Prophecy, embodied in Elijah, had also been fulfilled in Jesus. The Old Testament pointed to Christ in all its books, as the passage just quoted from Luke 24 explains.

The story of the Transfiguration is told in the setting of the Old Testament accounts of God's disclosure of himself. Jesus took his disciples up a high mountain, a place where in many cultures men have felt nearest to God. Mountains are venerated as the places where the gods live, like Greek gods on Mount Olympus or Hindu gods born in the snow-capped Himalayas. Moses received the law of God on Mount Sinai and went up into the clouds which covered the mountain to meet with God face to face, as a man converses with his friend. When Moses came down, his face was shining with the reflected glory of God, and he had to cover his face with a veil until the radiance faded. This account may look back to the prophet Ezekiel who described God's glory, his appearance and his presence in terms of shining light. God dwells in light unapproachable, we are told. It is a symbol of a fact we cannot measure or comprehend. The Jews used the symbol of light or fire to indicate that God was present, and also the clouds. So here in the Mount of Transfiguration a cloud comes down, a shining cloud, and the voice heard from the cloud must be the voice of God.

If we may translate this Jewish symbolism into our terms we may say that the three apostles received a disclosure that made them certain of Jesus' calling by God and special relationship to him. By the time the Gospel was written, the expression 'Son of God' applied to Jesus meant far more than it had meant to a Jew contemporary with Jesus. He would have used it to mean a really good man. Jesus, with his face shining like the sun and his garments luminous and dazzlingly white, is the revelation of God's nature in the teacher of Galilee. 'We beheld his glory, full of grace and truth' (John 1.14).

Peter had to learn the lesson, which Jesus had known from the beginning, that the divine glory was not something to be grasped and retained for yourself. If you have a great spiritual experience, it will probably be of short duration, and you have to find God's reality not only on the mountaintop, but in the hot and dusty plain as well. So the disciples are warned to tell no-one of what they had seen. They get to the foot of the mountain and are faced with a disturbing, even threatening scene. A father has brought his epileptic boy to Jesus to be healed. In Jesus' absence on the mountain he asks the disciples to cure his son, but they cannot. The indignant father, in his disappointment, expresses his sense of outrage just as Jesus arrives on the scene. The boy falls down in a fit, and Jesus heals him. The contrast between the peace of the mountain and the anger and noise of the crowd and the poor child was very great. God was there too, however, and his glory was shown in the compassion and love of Jesus as truly as in the shining glory on the mountain.

This vision, as Matthew calls it, of the transfigured Christ was to the first Christians the confirmation that their Lord had truly come from God, that he was God's Son, and that he fulfilled and completed God's disclosure of himself to his people Israel.

In the mid 5th century the Bishop of Rome, Leo the Great, preached on the Transfiguration on the eve of Lent 4. Leo's primary concern was right doctrine, so he uses the story to show how Peter at Caesarea Philippi first grasped the divine nature of Jesus when he called him the Son of the living God, and was then confused by the prophecy of all too human suffering and death. Leo thought that the Transfiguration happened to reassure Peter and the other two disciples, and to make them understand that hidden beneath the human nature of their master was the glory which came from his union with God. If they could grasp this truth, they could bear the bewilderment which would come to them when their Lord was crucified and killed. Leo believed that the Transfiguration was shown to them so that they could find the Cross bearable.

Leo says that the Transfiguration also shows the Church the kind of experience it will have to undergo if it is to share the glory of the risen Christ. Christians are united with Christ, and so with his glory and his victory, though this is normally hidden as it was in the case of their master. One of the texts Leo uses to reinforce this encouragement is Romans 8.18: 'For I consider that the sufferings of the present time are not worthy to be compared with the glory which shall be revealed.'

The experience of the disciples at the Transfiguration was an experience of faith which enabled them to look beyond the sufferings of this present time to the glory that shall be revealed. This faith in the reality and reliability of God gives us hope in every situation. Many Christians have lived lives of poverty or pain, and have neither made light of their troubles, or grumbled about them. They have endured and found in the sympathy and practical sharing of their fellows glimpses of the love of God. 'They have endured as seeing him who is invisible' (Hebrews 11.27). Corrie ten Boom in her book, *The Hiding Place*, tells us of such signs and reassurance, even in the terrible hardships and danger of Ravensbrook concentration camp during the war. There are many witnesses to this experience.

All of us have met people whose lives have a quality which marks them out from their fellows. All the people I have described in this book have this quality. They may be people who live solitary lives, like Julia Potts, or people under constant pressure because of their involvement in other people's suffering, like Archbishop Tutu and Mother Teresa, or they may be people working in industry, or carrying out the duties of family life. Such people seem to have a deep inner peace and to be centred in others, not in themselves. Nearly all of them give a good deal of time to prayer. They have to, if they are to remain faithful. Luther is said once to have explained that he was so busy that he had to spend at least three hours a day in prayer.

The quality of faith, hope and love seen in such people is the result of God working in them. These qualities are the fruits of the spirit, as Paul put it. They may not be so dramatic as the glory of Jesus on the holy mount, but more akin to the compassion which healed the epileptic boy at the foot of the mountain. All these qualities have one origin. They are demonstrations of the divine, working in and through our human nature. With most of us, the process of transfiguration by which our personalities are conformed to Christ is not regular and sustained, but irregular and interrupted. Lent is a time for honest scrutiny of ourselves, and the desire that we may live by the Spirit and not be mastered by our lower nature, as the

New English Bible translates Paul's word, the flesh. Paul uses this word in different ways, but in this context it means being influenced and controlled by the human environment in which we live, by the standards of a society that does not believe in God. For most of us the transformation from living in the flesh to living in the Spirit is a life-long movement, involving regress as well as progress.

In people who have not been aware of God until they have experienced a sudden conversion, the change may be spectacular, and cannot be explained away. It is clearly a fact. In Lent 1957 a mission was held in the diocese of Uganda. One mission team preached in the central prison in Kampala, and many prisoners were converted. A group of these prisoners was transferred not long afterwards to complete their sentences on a prison farm. Soon after arrival they complained to the authorities that there was no chapel, and that they had no place for daily prayers. The authorities promised to provide the materials if the prisoners would build the chapel in their spare time, which they did. Preparation classes for baptism and confirmation were soon in full swing, conducted like the daily worship, by the prisoners themselves, as there was no chaplain. Soon I was summoned to confirm about twenty prisoners, whom I found to be very well prepared. I noticed a really beautiful garden round the chapel, and was told by the superintendent of the prison that this was largely the work of one elderly man. This man had been an unco-operative and very bad tempered prisoner before, avoided as far as possible by the staff and his fellow prisoners. He had been converted during the mission, and his character had changed. He still was rather solitary in his habits, but as he did his gardening any prisoner who felt depressed or worried would seek him out, squat beside him as he worked, and share his troubles with him. The superintendent told me that the spiteful old man had become the greatest influence for happiness and harmony in the prison.

When Paul talks about the change brought about by God through faith in Jesus, he is clear that it is not self-induced, but the gift of God. 'For it is the God who said, "Let light shine out of darkness", who has shone in our hearts to give the light of the knowledge of the glory of God in the face of Christ.' (2 Corinthians 4.6 RSV) Paul knows that those who have come to faith and are capable of mental reflection on what has happened, will certainly realise that this was God's doing. He says, 'And we all, with unveiled face, beholding the glory of the Lord, are being changed into his likeness from one degree of glory to another' (2 Corinthians 3.18 RSV).

Paul was certainly not thinking of the Christians as a random collection of individuals. There could be nothing random in it because behind every conversion was the love of God working through the Spirit in that person's life. The Christians were organically connected with each other by their sharing in one Spirit. They were a fellowship, one body of Christ in which he was the active principle, using the body as the organ through which he continued his work.

We often hear it said in this country that a person's religion is their private affair. No blame attaches to those who are religious. If people like that sort of thing they are free to practise it, provided they do not interfere with others who are not religious. Such a way of thinking is foreign to the New Testament writers. They thought of people always in connection with their family or their tribe. The isolated individual was an unusual and sad case. So much of Paul's teaching, which we apply personally to ourselves as individuals, was addressed in the first place to the group of believers, the Church. It follows, therefore, that the first place in which we should expect to see the working of God's power is the congregation, rather than the individual believer. We find this taken for granted in much of the third world, where the old social structure of the extended family has not yet been broken down by the changes in the economic basis of society. This is the reason why the Church often grows by accession of family groups, rather than by individual conversion. In his splendid book, *Christianity Rediscovered*, Father Donovan tells of his mission to the Masai tribe in East Africa. He gave intensive instruction to a group of families who lived in one kraal. At the end of six months he invited them to decide whether or not they wished to become Christians and be baptised. They asked for baptism. Then Father Donovan started selecting those whom he considered ready for baptism, and others who needed further preparation. The elder of the group said that it was a question of all or none. It was true that some seemed to have less faith than others, but the others would have to make up for their friends' lack of faith. Some had not learned well, but the others would have to teach them. So none was refused. The whole community was baptised into the Church.

An anthropologist working among very similar cattle-tending nomads in Uganda once told me that the difference between Christian and non-Christian kraals was at once obvious when you visited them. The way of life was different in that worship was central to the life of the Christians, and their standards of cleanliness and happiness were different. This transformation, partial though it must always be, is the sign of God's working in the corporate life of the group.

All human communities show a dark side as well as a light side, and the Christian Church is no exception. Often we are inward looking, very concerned with our own domestic affairs, and not sensitive to the needs of the larger community in which we live. We are concerned with the maintenance and improvement of our own property more than anything else. We do not show a welcoming face to strangers, and we have little interest even in other Christian groups in the area. Sometimes we have a reputation, which may or may not be deserved, for back-biting and gossip. One function of our body is to enable us to be recognised by others. As Christ's body we are to be the means by which Christ is recognisable; instead we often obscure him. But there is a light side too, in almost every case. Although we often hide him rather than reveal him, yet there are many congregations whose life of care for those within and without its fellowship does show forth Christ. A small parish of backward class Christians in South India, not the Karali described in Chapter 2, was rent by disputes and quarrelling. One result of this was that very few people came to Communion for they realised they must not receive the sacrament unless they were in love and charity with one another. Something happened to these people. Enemies forgave each other and the corporate life was renewed. Small groups of men would meet at night after a day's work in the fields, and visit any in their part of the parish who were sick or in trouble. They would sing hymns and offer prayers, and take a little food from their own meagre resources as a present. Families who had been long estranged from the Church asked to be received back. When questioned why they wanted to return, two such families said it was because of the fellowship they saw in the life of the parish.

The Church reveals Christ's glory as much in its persistent effort to love as in its most splendid worship. The glory of God which shone from the face of Jesus on the holy mount, was the same glory that was reflected in the faces of the dying men in the stadium in Kabale.

Lent 5   The Victory of the Cross

Jesus and his disciples were on the road, going up to Jerusalem, Jesus leading the way; and the disciples were filled with awe, while those who followed behind were afraid. He took the Twelve aside and began to tell them what was to happen to him. 'We are now going to Jerusalem,' he said; 'and the Son of Man will be given up to the chief priests and the doctors of the law; they will condemn him to death and hand him over to the foreign power. He will be mocked and spat upon, flogged and killed; and three days afterwards, he will rise again.'

James and John, the sons of Zebedee, approached him and said, 'Master, we should like you to do us a favour.' 'What is it you want me to do?' he asked. They answered, 'Grant us the right to sit in state with you, one at your right and the other at your left.' Jesus said to them, 'You do not understand what you are asking. Can you drink the cup that I drink, or be baptised with the baptism I am baptised with?' 'We can', they answered. Jesus said, 'The cup that I drink you shall drink, and the baptism I am baptised with shall be your baptism; but to sit at my right or left is not for me to grant; it is for those to whom it has already been assigned.'

When the other ten heard this, they were indignant with James and John. Jesus called them to him and said, 'You know that in the world the recognised rulers lord it over their subjects, and their great men make them feel the weight of authority. That is not the way with you; among you, whoever wants to be great must be your servant, and whoever wants to be first must be the willing slave of all. For even the Son of Man did not come to be served but to serve, and give up his life as a ransom for many.'

(Mark 10. 32-45 NEB)

When we speak of the victory of the cross we are thinking of Jesus whose acceptance of suffering and death was the culmination of a life completely committed to God. Jesus was never free from conflict. His faith was always being tested. Many Christians have repeated in their lives the pattern Christ laid down. Janani Luwum was one of this company.

Janani was born in northern Uganda in 1924. His father had been one of the first in the Acholi tribe to become a Christian, and had worked as a catechist, caring for a small congregation. He supported himself by growing food crops and by the gifts in kind of his equally poor parishioners. His children could not go to school as there was no money for fees. So Janani herded goats in the bush until his early teens. Then he went to primary school, and proved a very bright pupil. There was no cash for him to continue his education. He got work as an unlicensed teacher in a small, unregistered school, and eventually saved enough money to go to a teacher training college for lower grade teachers. He passed the exams, and then felt called to the ministry. He was accepted and ordained deacon in 1955.

Janani worked as a pastor and was so conspicuously able he was sent for further training to England. After his return in 1966 he became Provincial Secretary of the Church of Uganda. He was one of the Archbishop of Canterbury's consultants at the 1968 Lambeth Conference, and soon after was elected Bishop of Northern Uganda, and then in 1974 Archbishop of Uganda.

This kind of career might have turned many people's heads, but Janani took all the changes in his circumstances and environment in his stride. I think he was entirely without ambition for himself, and he had learned that when God calls his servants to some new work, he gives also the ability to do that work. So Janani was unfussed and serene, whether he was talking to children in a village school, or representing his church in the Anglican Consultative Council or on the Central Committee of the World Council of Churches. He was always calm, always listened to anyone who came to him, always courteous and thinking of other people's interests and hopes. He had a great sense of humour and laughed easily.

In 1976 I saw him at the Anglican Consultative Council meeting in Trinidad. I was greatly troubled by the reports of atrocities in Uganda under President Amin's rule. I asked Janani and the other two Ugandan representatives about it. He told me that a military regime could not be judged by the standards of a democratic government. He added, with a smile of confidence and reassurance, 'Don't be worried. God is in control. One thing is clear. The Church must not compromise truth. Perhaps some of us may be killed, but it is all right. We are in God's hands.'

A few months later, in February 1977, we heard of Janani's death. The Anglican Bishops had sent a letter to President Amin, asking him to control his security forces who were robbing, raping and killing ordinary law-abiding citizens with no cause. The country was living in fear. This careful and restrained statement was read as treasonable. The Bishops were summoned to the army headquarters in Kampala where, in the presence of invited visitors and a strong army detachment, they were stood in the hot sun for several hours, and harangued about disloyalty. Then Janani was taken by soldiers to see the President. Two other bishops tried to follow him, but were knocked back by rifle butts. As he was taken away Janani turned to his brother bishops, smiled at them and said, 'Do not be afraid. I see God's hand in this.'

After interrogation Janani was taken to the security police headquarters. Stripped to his underclothes, he was pushed into a room already holding about forty prisoners. They recognised him, and one asked for his blessing. A soldier, for some reason, restored Janani's purple cassock and cross. He prayed for them all, and blessed them. One of the men who was a prisoner in that room told me long afterwards that a great calm

86

and peace came to them all, and their despair lifted. Then Janani was taken out and shot, still in his cassock. The government report to the world press was that the Archbishop had been killed in a car accident.

The following Sunday was to have been the funeral at the Cathedral. A new grave had been dug, next to the grave of Bishop Hannington, martyred in 1885, but the government refused to hand over the body, and forbade any memorial service. So the great crowd who filled the cathedral had their Eucharist. At the end, as they came out of church and saw the empty grave, they started singing Easter hymns. The retired Archbishop Erica Sabiti, who had visited Janani the night before he died and had prayed with him, told the people that Janani had been sure he was going to be killed. Archbishop Sabiti said that even if all the bishops were killed, God was still there, and the Church could not be destroyed. The sound of the singing was heard a long way away, and many people came up the hill to join them, from the Roman Catholic churches as well as from Anglican congregations. As a direct result of Janani's death, the Church went forward with renewed hope and confidence.

The Alternative Service Book theme for this Sunday, the Victory of the Cross, is not well exemplified by the set readings. They point to the contrast between the world's standard of success and achievement and Christ's. This Sunday is often called Passion Sunday. That is a good name, if we keep in our mind the original meaning of the words suffering, which is English, and passion, which is Latin. Both words have the same root meaning. It is the acceptance of what comes, the allowing something to happen, which for Christians who believe in God, is not a counsel of despair but of hope. The theme has been spelled out in Chapter 4.

The introductory words of the Gospel cast a vivid light on what followed. Jesus has decided to go up to Jerusalem for the national festival of Passover, but the disciples are not looking forward to visiting the people and the city. For a Jew, Jerusalem was the city of peace, the centre of their national life, the dwelling place of God himself. Jerusalem was also a dangerous place for anyone who was not a wholehearted conformist, as the holy city of Coum in Iran is at the present day. Jerusalem was filled with rival sects and fierce disputations about the law of God. The Jewish leaders were scrupulous in their observance of the law, but unscrupulous in the way they dealt with anyone who appeared to challenge their authority. We are told elsewhere that when Jesus came within sight of the city he wept over it, because it was not putting its faith in God but in itself, as a place whose choice by God guaranteed its permanence. This was a false faith, and the old prophets had already seen that it would lead to the destruction of the holy city. Jesus himself observed that the prophets, who had spoken in God's name, had often been rejected and killed in this most religious city.

So, Mark tells us, Jesus led the way to Jerusalem. The disciples followed, loyally enough, but were confused and full of questioning. At this stage, apparently, they were not frightened and fearful of what might happen, but they were apprehensive. In his

Gospel John tells us that when Jesus decided to go up to Jerusalem to comfort Mary and Martha when Lazarus died, the disciples tried to persuade him not to go. He would not listen, and Thomas said with resignation, 'We must go too, even if it means dying with him.' The other people in the company were plain scared. Jesus' disciples were country folk. They marvelled at the great buildings of the city, and probably felt overwhelmed by such surroundings. They also had a sense of foreboding as they felt hostility towards their master all around them.

According to Mark, Jesus took the twelve disciples, and told them what would happen to him. The careful breakdown of the Passion of Jesus in six separate stages reads like an account written after the Resurrection, describing what had actually happened. Mark tells us that this was the third time Jesus had warned his disciples of the fate that awaited him. It seems unlikely that Mark is claiming that Jesus knew every detail in advance, but he might have done. We cannot be sure. Although this prophecy of doom ends with a prediction of his resurrection, the disciples were not greatly comforted because they did not know what this meant. When Jesus did rise from the dead, it took them all completely by surprise.

The story which follows is not an obvious sequel to what has gone before. Luke apparently felt this, and transposed it to a different occasion in his narrative. In this Gospel we are told that James and John, the two fishermen whom Jesus called from their work with their father, approach him and ask for the two most important places in Jesus' kingdom. They do not qualify this request. They take it for granted that Jesus is going to set up a Jewish kingdom and reign as its king. They do not pause to reflect that Jesus himself has given them no grounds for this assumption. They have misunderstood completely what Jesus is doing. His warnings of coming suffering and death have fallen on deaf ears. They will not hear what they do not want to hear.

Jesus' answer can neither be a plain yes or no, because either might add to their misunderstanding. He asks them if they would be able to drink his cup or share his baptism. The Old Testament speaks of a cup of joy and gladness, but also of the cup of the wrath of God, and this seems to be the implication of Jesus' words. Both cup and baptism point to suffering and death. James and John reply that they can share his cup and his baptism. Jesus confirms that they will do so, but their actual request can be answered only by God. God has a purpose for everyone, and he alone knows who will be given the greatest honour in his kingdom. These words affirm the unchanging purpose of God for men and women, what the Old Testament calls his steadfast love and the New Testament calls grace.

It is not easy to find appropriate words to express clearly such ideas. When the Bible was written in the Luganda language the only word the translators could find for grace was *ekisa*. This word was formerly used for the arbitrary favour of a king or chief. On a whim he might suddenly give a person a gift, or some honour. This was called *ekisa*. But his mood could change to anger, and his *ekisa*, his favour, might last only for a moment. In fact, the Luganda word so used in the Bible gave an impression then, though it has acquired a Christian meaning since, that contrary to the Bible witness, God might be as unreliable as a chief.

Jesus will not promise anything suddenly to James and John, however hard they press him. Their bid for status was naturally resented by the others, who were probably just as ambitious, but less quick witted. By the time Matthew's Gospel was written, the Christians felt ashamed that two of their apostolic leaders had shown such barefaced self interest, and so it was said that it was not the brothers who made the request to Jesus, but their mother on her sons' behalf. Luke does not mention the incident at all.

Jesus was now faced with an angry group of disciples, all thinking of what they would get out of the coming kingdom, and none stopping to check their fantasies with what Jesus had actually said. Jesus tells them that his kingdom does not follow worldly patterns. They can see in the world how rulers function, how they support their own power and status in various ways, and make people feel the weight of their authority. In the world a man's standing and greatness are measured by the service he receives from others. In God's kingdom it is measured by the service he gives to others. In the world such an opinion is quite literally nonsense. If anyone says such things he will be treated with contempt as a fool. If anyone tries to live like that, many will be deeply suspicious of his motives. In a certain English approved school a few of the staff kept open house for the boys who had been sent there for criminal offences. But the boys responded with suspicion. What's he getting out of it? Where's the catch?

Jesus goes on to say that he, Son of Man, did not come to be served but to serve, and to give his life as a ransom for many. We read this Gospel as, in our attempt to enter into the meaning of Christ's passion, we go with him to Jerusalem. We know what awaited him there. At the time the disciples did not know. The six stage prediction of these events, put into the mouth of Jesus in this Gospel, was fulfilled in fact. The word ransom implies that Jesus knew what he was doing. God's will to save the world would lead him through obedience to the complete offering of himself in death. The shepherd would have to lay down his life for the sheep, the friend for his friends. During the Maccabean wars at the end of the second century B.C the idea of offering one's life for the nation was understood by the Jews and described by the word ransom.

If the word ransom is meant to remind the reader of the suffering servant of Isaiah 53, with its reference especially to dying for many, then Jesus' thinking, or that of the early Church, is quite clear, for the servant does lay down his life for many. The scholars are uncertain about this connection. Many think there is no such reference, as I indicated above.

Certainly the Gospels are agreed that Jesus went up to Jerusalem to face suffering and death, and was aware of what would confront him. It is little wonder that Paul wrote to the Corinthian Christians that his preaching of Christ crucified was a stumbling block to the Jews, and folly to the non Jews (1 Corinthians 1.23). The consequences of the Gospel story are in such contradiction to the received ideas of our society, as they were to first century society, that they are dismissed without consideration as nonsense. A first century graffito survives, scrawled in mockery of the Christians, showing a man on a cross with a donkey's head. That is how absurd our faith often appears to the outsider. This is understandable, but as Paul says, to us who are being saved from sin and conformity to the world's standards, Christ on the cross is the power of God and the wisdom of God.

A servant works for his wages. Christ came to serve humankind not for wages, but out of love. His service was motivated by his own nature, which was concerned for the welfare of others more than for his own. This is what Christians mean by love. John says that Jesus loved his own who were in the world, to the end. The word used for 'to the end' can mean completely, i.e. until death, until the end of life. He gave his life as a ransom for many.

In the Old Testament, especially in the Psalms, God is constantly begged to fight for his people, and to go out with their armies into battle. He is the Lord of the armies, who will destroy the enemies of his people, and give his people their lands. There is every support in the Bible for Israel's stand against her Arab neighbours, and for her prompt retaliation to violence against her. Jesus, however, teaches a different way. 'You have heard that it was said, "An eye for an eye and a tooth for a tooth." But I say to you, Do not resist one who is evil. But if any one strikes you on the right cheek, turn to him the other also; and if any one would sue you and take your coat, let him have your cloak as well. . . . You have heard that it was said, "You shall love your neighbour and hate your enemy". But I say to you, Love your enemies and pray for those who persecute you, so that you may be sons of your Father who is in heaven; for he makes his sun rise on the evil and on the good, and sends rain on the just and on the unjust' (Matthew 5.38ff). This teaching sounds quite impossible to follow, but Jesus acted as he taught. His method of dealing with evil was to face it without resistance, and accept all it did to him, never being diverted from his trust in God or his care for those who were so injuring him. He was never seduced or compromised by their evil. He overcame evil by good, hatred by love, but the cost was his own life. This is a strange way of victory, by conquering evil in men and women, not destroying the men and women themselves.

It is clear from the New Testament that the first Christians came to believe that the suffering and death of Jesus was the way God had chosen to counter sin and destroy its power. This was not an abstract or theoretical concept. It was lived out in thousands of Christian lives. Christians have never been allowed to seek martyrdom, but from the earliest times martyrs have been honoured as those whose lives have not been wasted, but who have in some way made a contribution to the defeat of evil and liberation of mankind. In our own century there have been mass martyrdoms on an unthinkable and horrendous scale, as in the holocaust of six million Jews in Nazi Germany. It is very difficult to see how their enforced martyrdom contributed to the welfare of the human race. It seems to us unrelieved tragedy. But it remains true that Christians have always believed that self-sacrifice, if necessary to death, is a means of working with God for his purpose.

The death of Jesus was seen as the victory of God over evil. On the Emmaus road the risen but unrecognised Christ said to the two disconsolate disciples who told him of their desolation at their master's death, 'O foolish men, was it not necessary that the Christ should suffer these things and enter into his glory?' (Luke 24.25ff RSV). The way to glory is through suffering. When John reports the conversation of Jesus in the upper room before he was betrayed, he says that Jesus used the word glory several times in connection with his death. The hour had come for the Father to be glorified through the self-giving of his son. As he had said before, when the Greeks wanted to see him, if he was lifted up, in death on a cross, he would draw all men to himself.

As Jesus glorified God by his death, so we who are united to Christ by faith, must live lives of obedience, so that whether by life or death we may bring glory to God. 'Jesus said to Peter, "Truly, truly, I say to you, when you were young, you girded yourself and walked where you would; but when you are old, you will stretch out your hands, and another will gird you and carry you where you do not wish to go." This he said to show by what death he was to glorify God' (John 21.18ff RSV). An eye-witness account of the death of the Uganda martyrs at Namugongo, a few miles from Kampala, on 3 July, 1886, is still extant. Forty men and youths had been arrested for their Christian faith. They were marched from the king's palace to this place of execution. They were imprisoned in small, dark huts, each in his own hut under guard. When after some days they were brought out to be prepared for death by burning, there was great jubilation and excitement as they recognised each other, and congratulated each other on remaining faithful until that day. They sang hymns and submitted to being bound in bundles of dry reeds, and being stacked together on a great pile of firewood. When the fire was lit, they still sang through the flames until, one by one, they succumbed to the heat and smoke. They glorified God by their deaths. Half were Roman Catholics, now canonised, and the others Anglicans. From the time of these martyrdoms the two Churches have grown until the great majority of Ugandans are now Christians. In 1984 government soldiers came to Namugongo, where there is an Anglican clergy school, and shot the principal and another teacher in front of the students, for no known reason. He also, like his predecessors a hundred years before, died praying for those who killed him.

Christ's victory over evil is seen whenever men and women live lives of service to their fellows, not thinking of their own profit or advantage. He overcomes not only our natural selfishness and self regard, but our fears for the present and the future. Few of us are likely to be called to sacrifice on such an heroic scale. In normal times heroics are not called for, but steady faithfulness. This may be in the area of service or witness, or in the daily task of caring for our own folk in our own home. Sometimes we are reticent when we ought to speak. Sometimes we avoid situations when we might be useful to someone else, because it would involve inconvenience and time we can ill afford to spend. Whatever our circumstances, man's chief end remains the same, to glorify God and enjoy him for ever.

The Church, too, is called to live for God's glory. We often mistake maintenance for mission, as if our main task is to preserve the Church as we have known it, and hold firmly to the old tried ways in which our fathers have walked. The Church belongs to God. It is not our private property, a kind of social club. The life of the Church has to be measured by the values Christ taught and embodied. The Church must always be re-formed in the light of the Gospel. Jesus lived and died for the glory of God. Still he wishes to use his body, the Church, in the same obedience. It is easy to write these things. To attempt to conform the life of the Church at every level to Christ is a demanding task that never ends.

In his life and his death Archbishop Janani Luwum showed that the victory of the cross is still powerfully at work. Millions of others all down the ages have lived in its light, and, paradoxically, shared its joy.

Lent 6   The Way of the Cross

Jesus and his disciples were nearing Jerusalem; and when they reached Bethphage at the Mount of Olives, Jesus sent two of them with these instructions: 'Go to the village opposite, where you will at once find a donkey tethered with her foal beside her; untie them, and bring them to me. If anyone speaks to you, say, ''Our Master needs them''; and he will let you take them at once.' This was to fulfil the prophecy which says, 'Tell the daughter of Zion, ''Here is your king, who comes to you in gentleness, riding on an ass, riding on the foal of a beast of burden.'''

The disciples went and did as Jesus had directed, and brought the donkey and her foal; they laid their cloaks on them, and Jesus mounted. Crowds of people carpeted the road with their cloaks, and some cut branches from the trees to spread in his path. Then the crowd that went ahead and the others that came behind raised the shout: 'Hosanna to the Son of David! Blessings on him who comes in the name of the Lord! Hosanna in the heavens!'

When he entered Jerusalem the whole
city went wild with excitement. 'Who is
this?' people asked, and the crowd replied,
'This is the prophet Jesus, from Nazareth in
Galilee.'

Jesus then went into the temple and
drove out all who were buying and selling
in the temple precincts; he upset the tables
of the money-changers and the seats of the
dealers in pigeons; and said to them, 'Scripture says, ''My house shall be called a house
of prayer''; but you are making it a robbers'
cave.'

(Matthew 21. 1.13 NEB)

Anyone who saw the film *Gandhi* will remember the
brief and rather surprising appearance of a young
English priest, wearing an English suit and a clerical
collar, even in that hot and sticky climate. This was
Charles Freer Andrews. Charlie Andrews was born in
1871. He took a good degree at Cambridge, and was
elected a fellow of Pembroke College. He was ordained
and went with the Cambridge Mission to Delhi to teach
at St Stephen's College in 1904. There he made a close
friendship with the Indian Vice Principal, a man of
deep Christian faith, and already involved in the
concern for Indian culture and Indian identity as a
nation. Andrews accepted these ideas enthusias-
tically, and met some of the men who were to lead the
movement to Indian independence. He travelled to Fiji
and other places where Indian labour was being
exploited, and fought for the rights of the labourers.
Eventually, he went to live with Rabindranath Tagore

at his ashram in Shantiniketan. Here he met again M. K. Gandhi, with whom he had worked in South Africa when investigating the condition of Indian indentured labourers. He became Gandhi's close friend, completely trusted by him. From that time he lived and worked with Indian nationalists and, although he was sometimes used by Government to explain positions or mediate between them and his friends, he was mistrusted by most British people in India, although they had never met him. In spite of books like *What I Owe to Christ* and *Christ in the Silence*, many Christians assumed Andrews had compromised his Christian faith. In 1938 I was staying in the Nilgiri Hills with a young missionary, just posted there. Andrews asked if he could come to stay with us, but the senior missionary, whose permission we had to ask, turned down our request. He said that Andrews was a traitor to his country, and an apostate from Christianity. I had to tell Andrews. I still remember his sadness, without a trace of anger, as he told me that the Viceroy had three times pressed him to accept the gold Kaiser-i-Hind medal, as a mark of gratitude for his reconciling and mediating work between nationalist Indians and the British raj. Andrews had not accepted the honour in case it caused any misunderstanding among his Indian friends. As for apostasy, he told me that many Indians believed that his initials C.F. stood for Christian Faith.

Andrews followed the way of the Cross in more ways than patiently bearing lies and misrepresentation from British people serving in India. He lived a most ascetic life in Indian village conditions, as if it were his natural environment. I was told that his bedder, in his rooms at Pembroke where his Fellow's set was reserved for him even though he was rarely there, complained that Andrews only had two shirts. He would wash one and leave it to dry on the radiator while he wore the other, and then exchange them. On one occasion he had been in college only a day or so, when he heard of some trouble affecting Indian labour in Fiji. He spent all the money he had, buying a ticket, and set off at once. A friend lent him a raincoat, for it was raining and Andrews had no coat. The friend never saw his raincoat again.

He lived tirelessly for other people. No one in any kind of need was outside his concern. He was greatly loved by Indians. During Gandhiji's illness, Andrews was constantly with him, and the Press reported that he would sing Gandhi's favourite hymn during night prayers, 'When I survey the wondrous Cross'. Andrews never counted the cost to himself of any-thing he did. He died in 1940. In a public statement Gandhi said, 'Not only England, not only India, have lost a true servant, but humanity. . . . I have not known a better man or a truer Christian than C. F. Andrews.' If the way of the cross is concerned with losing your own self for Christ's sake, then Andrews walked steadfastly in that way.

Mabel Knowles had been born into a rich banker's family. She grew up with everything she could poss-ibly need, and at the right time 'came out' into society, as was the custom of her class. Then came the First World War. Her family home in the country was turned into a hospital for wounded soldiers. Mabel and her sisters, young women in their early twenties, nursed in the hospital, and came into close contact with a class of people they had never encountered before. At some point in this story Mabel's faith became the most important thing in life to her. She began to feel she could not return to her former way of life; morally good and entertaining as it was, it no longer satisfied her. She bought a small, terraced house in a street near the Victoria docks, in Custom House, London, in the parish of St Luke. She took over a small mission church, St Albans, and began a ministry which was to last many years. She did not feel competent to preach, so she employed and paid for a series of Church Army Captains and Sisters, and lay readers. The clergy of St Luke's came to give the sacraments.

At that time there was deep poverty in the area, bad housing conditions, much unemployment. There was one street down which no policeman would ever venture alone. So Mabel Knowles bought a vacant lot, put up an old army hut, and opened it as a church. It soon became a centre for the children, and the atmosphere of the street began to change.

Mabel Knowles was generous to a fault, and her workers were sometimes embarrassed and annoyed by it. They were angry with the imposters who deceived her with their hard-luck stories, to which she would always respond with help. She could be seen every day, with a basket on her arm containing food or little luxuries for the sick. In those days there was no welfare state, no public assistance and no supplementary benefit. She visited them all, undeterred by the rats and the bugs and lack of sanitation, which were usual in some streets. She herself appeared to live only on bread, butter and tea. She looked fragile, but was always cheerful and appreciative of any kindness she saw.

For some time Mabel went up to the West End at regular intervals, to help with a Christian group called Reveille, which she had started. The members came to their meetings in evening dress, a far cry from her friends in Custom House. She took one holiday a year, and buried herself in the country, writing adventure books, very moral indeed, for teenagers. This was to raise money for her work, which needed a yearly injection of cash.

Mabel Knowles had no concern at all with herself, or her reputation. She was wholly concerned with the people she served. There was not a trace of condescension or patronising in her. She lived by and for love.

C. F. Andrews and Mabel Knowles did not plan their lives in advance. They responded to the challenges and opportunities of each day and did what they believed God had given them to do. In obeying God they followed Jesus Christ. Jesus' obedience led him to surrender himself to the authorities, without any attempt to fight against them or to escape. This obedience led directly to his death on the cross. The decisive step was taken when he rode into Jerusalem on what we call Palm Sunday.

Jesus' disciples had tried to dissuade him from attending the festival in the Temple at Jerusalem, but his mind was made up, and he set out. The disciples followed him, though Thomas is reported as saying with unwilling resignation, 'Let us also go, that we may die with him' (John 11.16 RSV). As they came to the end of their journey south they approached the Mount of Olives. Jesus sent two of his disciples to a nearby village where he had arranged to borrow a donkey to ride on the last stage of his journey. There are discrepancies in the Gospel accounts. Matthew says firmly that two animals were to be brought, so that the Jewish prophecy would be fulfilled (Zechariah 9.9 RSV). 'Rejoice greatly, O daughter of Zion! Shout aloud, O daughter of Jerusalem! Lo, your king comes to you; triumphant and victorious is he, humble and riding on an ass, on a colt, the foal of an ass.' It was a common figure of speech in Hebrew poetry to repeat something in slightly different words, and Luke and Mark both understood the prophecy in this way and mention only one animal. For Matthew, Jesus' action was the sign that he was the King for whom they were waiting.

It seems as if Jesus' disciples recognised the sign, because they provided cloaks for a saddle and surrounded Jesus as he rode over the summit of the Mount of Olives, and saw Jerusalem spread out in front of him, with the dome of the Temple shining in the sun above the roofs of the houses. A wave of excitement must have rushed through them, and it was disconcerting and unexpected when Jesus' response to the sight was to weep.

It seems reasonable to think that on other occasions Jesus walked down the hill, over the river, and up the road into the holy city, like anyone else, inconspicuous and unrecognised. Now he made himself conspicuous

104

and was recognised by many as the prophet who had taught and healed in the villages. They shouted in excitement and broke branches off trees, and waved them as they greeted him as the descendant of David, coming in the name of the Lord. They shouted slogans which were at the same time a prayer to God to save his people and a political declaration. Naturally the children joined in, and followed Jesus and his friends, waving branches. I was always reminded of those children when I saw boys in Uganda riding back home after their confirmation service, laughing and calling out to each other, with sprigs of leaves decorating the handlebars of their bicycles.

All this may have been a demonstration of local loyalty as much as anything else. When the townspeople asked the shouting demonstrators who the man was whom they were acclaiming they said with pride that it was Jesus, the prophet of Nazareth in Galilee. The Jewish leaders were apparently not alarmed by the demonstration. They told Jesus to make his disciples control the children, but they did not call out their own police, or the Roman troops standing by in Fort Antonia, in case of disturbance at the Festival. It did not seem to them important or significant.

The incident must, however, have raised the hopes of the disciples, even though the small scale of the response to Jesus must have disappointed them. Perhaps they thought that Jesus was about to declare himself the national liberator all pious Jews prayed for, but this hope was to be unfulfilled, though they returned to it at the Ascension (Acts 1.6). The meaning of the sign Jesus gave was not plain and clear. It was like his parables, understood by those who had eyes to see and ears to hear, but not at once obvious to others. Matthew says that when they reached the city the whole town was moved. If that had been literally true the alarm would certainly have sounded. Probably it is as a man says to another in the course of an argument, '*Everybody* knows that.' Matthew probably means that a great number of people was interested in knowing what the excitement was about. Jesus had given his sign, though few understood its meaning.

According to Mark's account Jesus went into the Temple after his arrival in the city, and looked round, then he went back to the village of Bethany. Matthew says that Jesus did not go home at once to his friends, he gave a second sign. He went into the precincts of the Temple, where commercial business was carried on. They did not sell souvenirs, but the items necessary for worship. There were animals for sacrifice, ranging from heifers to pigeons. The examination of sacrificial animals was strict, and it was clearly more sensible to buy certified animals at the Temple itself than to bring your sacrifice with you, with the risk that, after a long journey it might not pass the test as an unblemished animal, fit to offer to the Lord. Of course, the animals were expensive and the Temple merchants had a monopoly of the trade. All coming as pilgrims had to offer a gold coin, struck expressly for this use. No other was accepted. So everyone had to change their own currency to obtain this special coin and, human nature being what it is, the exchange rate was probably high.

Jesus' action in releasing tethered animals, tipping over the moneychangers' tables, and lashing around him in anger with a piece of rope, driving the sellers and buyers out of the precinct, is usually taken as a protest against extortion, against using things destined to honour God as a means of personal profit. Jesus quoted two Old Testament passages: 'My house shall be called a house of prayer, but you are making it a robbers' cave.' This is a conflation of Isaiah 56.7 and Jeremiah 7.11. The word robbers gives support to the idea that Jesus was angry at the merchants' greed. This may or may not be so. An alternative explanation is that Jesus was deliberately giving the Jews another sign. Just as his entry on the donkey that day was seen as fulfilling Zechariah's prophesy of the coming of the King, so this forceful action of Jesus could have reminded them of the prophesy in Malachi 3. 1-2, of the Lord coming to his temple to cleanse it. Both actions were signs of a new order superseding the old. The Kingdom of God had come in Jesus, God was in their midst. The old was passing away, the new had come. The story of these events was written down long after the resurrection, and only then were the disciples able to see something of the meaning of these signs and of their implications for the life of the individual believer, of the Church, and of Society as a whole. Then they realised (John 2. 19-21) that the old Temple was to be replaced by a different kind of temple, in which God dwelt among men. This was the Church, the congregation of believers in Christ, who had become a living temple by the indwelling of the Spirit. Jesus said to the woman at the well, 'Believe me, the hour is coming when neither on this mountain or in Jerusalem will you worship the Father. But the hour is coming, and now is, when the true worshippers will worship the Father in spirit and truth' (John 4. 21,23 RSV). 'You are built upon the foundation laid by the apostles and prophets, and Christ Jesus himself is the foundation-stone. In him the whole building is bonded together and grows into a holy temple of the Lord. In him you too are being built with all the rest into a spiritual dwelling for God' (Ephesians 2. 20-22 NEB). The sign Jesus was giving when he cleansed the Temple was that the old had been superceded by the new disclosure of God's will in Jesus.

Matthew does not describe how Jesus wept when he saw the city of Jerusalem spread out before him. Luke gives us the story. I quote it here because it exposes the conflict between the ideas of popular religion and Jesus' own understanding of God. This conflict culminated in Jesus death on the cross. 'When he drew near and saw the city he wept over it saying, ''Would that even today you knew the things that make for peace! But now they are hid from your eyes''' (Luke 19. 41-42 RSV). Jesus, in Luke's account, went on to prophesy the destruction of the Holy City.

The destruction of Jerusalem was inevitable because the people did not practise the way of life which results in Shalom, peace. This peace is the will of God for humankind. It includes physical well-being, sufficient food and shelter, and social well-being with just and impartial government. This implies absence of strife, and the use of resources of every kind for the common good. The inescapable condition of Shalom is, in Hebrew thought, obedience to God and his laws.

The prophets were direct in their condemnation of those who regarded God as bound by his covenant to bless his people whether or not they obeyed him. The Temple which symbolised God's presence with them was in itself no guarantee of Shalom if they did not keep their side of the covenant. 'Thus says the Lord of hosts, the God of Israel, Amend your ways and your doings, and I will let you dwell in this place. Do not trust in these deceptive words: "This is the temple of the LORD, the temple of the LORD, the temple of the LORD"' (Jeremiah 7. 3,4 RSV). Like the prophets before him, Jesus saw the consequences of their wrong attitudes and actions, and wept, because he loved his nation. 'Oh Jerusalem, Jerusalem, killing the prophets and stoning those who are sent to you! How often would I have gathered your children together as a hen gathers her brood under her wings, and you would not! Behold, your house is forsaken and desolate. For I tell you, you will not see me again, until you say, "Blessed is he who comes in the name of the Lord"'.

'Jesus left the temple and was going away, when his disciples came to point out to him the buildings of the Temple. But he answered them, "You see all these, do you not? Truly, I say to you, there will not be left one stone upon another, that will not be thrown down"' (Matthew 23.37 24.2 RSV). Like the prophets before him, Jesus emphasised that God required righteousness more than all the observances of religion. The priests, who were also the rulers of the people, felt threatened by Jesus, just as their forebears had felt threatened by the prophets. 'The chief priests and the Pharisees gathered the council, and said, "What are we to do? For this man performs many signs. If we let him go on thus, everyone will believe in him, and the

Romans will come and destroy both our holy place and our nation." But one of them, Caiaphas, who was high priest that year, said to them, "You know nothing at all; you do not understand that it is expedient for you that one man should die for the people, and that the whole nation should not perish"' (John 11. 47-50 RSV).

As in Holy Week we reflect on the consequences to Jesus of his convictions, we have to apply his teaching to our own situation. The account of Jesus' clash with the Jewish authorities suggests that the preservation of national identity was their supreme objective. There is anxiety about this in contemporary Britain, but it is not the main concern of most people. Their main concern is making money or maintaining their present standard of living. A man is judged successful if he increases his wealth and possessions. His acceptance by society is not prejudiced by the way in which he acquired his money. An enterprise is not judged to be successful unless it is profitable in money terms. The excellence of its products or its social value to the community are not the criteria by which it is judged. Just as money is taken as the measure of success for individuals, so it is the basis of the philosophy of some political groups. It seems to determine policies which decide the amount of national income to be spent on public services like health and education, public transport and the social services. Money is sometimes considered more important than persons. I am not suggesting that good stewardship of the nation's resources is wrong, it is clearly right and proper. If however money becomes the all important factor in the decisions of individual or national life it becomes a god. Paul warns us that inordinate greed is idolatry, the worship of a false God. Jesus warned his hearers that it is not possible to serve God and Mammon. The word used in Greek means a 'slave', one who is completely obedient to his master. In the materialistic culture of our own western world we are called constantly to identify the God whom we are in fact serving. An African priest from Uganda was present at a lunch party in Minneapolis, U.S.A., given by wealthy businessmen to some of the delegates at the Anglican Congress held there in 1954. After a very good lunch the hosts and their guests were gazing out at the city from their dining room high up in a skyscraper. The tall buildings round them spoke of immense wealth. One of the businessmen turned to the priest and asked him what he thought of America. The priest replied simply and immediately, 'It is a very needy country, isn't it?' The response of his host to that is not recorded. It was plain that the African was not trying to be funny or clever. The Bible is quite clear that worship of a false God is the root of all evil, but it always acknowledges that Creation is in itself good, and all material things may be used in constructive ways. It is the abuse of a thing which is destructive; no created thing can be put in the place of God.

Probably the African priest's reaction to the material wealth he saw around him, and his sense of deep spiritual poverty in the country was excused by his American friends as caused by his ignorance of the real world. An American Christian who made a similar statement might well have been written off as a crank. We do not like people who do not conform to

111

the values of our society. When Francis of Assisi stripped off his rich clothes and gave them back to his father, saying that from that moment he would depend only on God, probably not only his relatives and neighbours, but the bishop himself, thought that Francis was mad. Christians have often had to be fools in the eyes of the world for Christ's sake, because he overturned the world's assumptions about wealth and position. He said to his disciples, 'You know that those who are supposed to rule over the Gentiles lord it over them, and their great men exercise authority over them. But it shall not be so among you; but whoever would be great among you must be your servant, and whoever would be first among you must be slave of all. For the Son of man also came not to be served but to serve, and to give his life as a ransom for many' (Mark 10. 42-45 RSV).

All through Holy Week Jesus' enemies listened to every word he said publicly, hoping to get evidence on which he could be charged. Hatred and hostility mounted.

Jesus was, in fact, quite right, if he spoke, as Matthew reports him, about the destruction of the city. In A.D. 70 the Romans razed the old city to the ground and destroyed the temple. All that remains is part of the podium on which the temple was built. The immense stones of the relic are now called the wailing wall, the nearest the present day Jews can get to the great temple of Jesus' day.

John tells us that when Jesus spoke of the destruction of the Temple and his power to rebuild it in three days, he was speaking about his body (John 2.21 RSV). As we have seen, the Church, the group of believers was thought of by Christian writers as the body of Christ, the new temple of God, built on Jesus and his apostles. This temple can also be destroyed. It is a sign of the Kingdom, not itself God's Kingdom. Where the Church has conformed to the values of its contemporary world it has sometimes, as in the churches overrun by Muslim invaders in North Africa and Asia Minor, been almost entirely destroyed. We get our identity and our values from Christ in our baptism, not from our particular contemporary culture. We have to examine ourselves about our lifestyle, and the extent to which we have allowed ourselves to be conformed to the secular culture whose God is not the God and Father of our Lord Jesus Christ.

There is no one rule of life statutory for all Christian men and women. Each of us has to discover by prayer and quiet waiting on God, with the advice and counsel of other Christians, how we are to apply our faith to life. As long as the world, human society, is guided and governed by aims and principles which are opposed to those we see in Christ, we have no option but to be non-conformist. Paul told his friends they were not to conform to the world but to be transformed by the renewing of their minds. We are in this world, living in our own societies, but our first loyalty is to Christ. When we are true to him we may be seen by our fellow-men and women to be a threat, as eccentric or as mad. Paul expressed this when he said that he had decided to preach about Christ, Christ crucified on the cross, which will be a stumbling block to Jews and sheer nonsense to the Greeks, even though it was to be to the Christians the source of

113

wisdom and peace. Every Christian has to work out his own rule of life in obedience to Christ, so does every congregation.

Charlie Andrews and Mabel Knowles did this all their lives. They did not judge or reject the people who belonged to their past, they continued to love them, but they were led into a different style of life by accepting the calls which came to them. In Andrews' case it resulted in much political involvement. In the case of Miss Knowles it led to a life of unseen and undramatic service, with no recognition or reward except the grateful appreciation of many people. For our Lord himself this life of obedience took him at last to Good Friday. He accepted all that came to him, all that was done to him "with fortitude, patience and joy" (Colossians 1,12 NEB) and showed on the cross the full extent of his love.

> 'Almighty God,
> whose most dear Son went not up to joy
>   but first he suffered pain,
> and entered not into glory before he was
> crucified:
> mercifully grant that we, walking in the
> way of the cross,
> may find it none other than the way of life
> and peace;
> through Jesus Christ our Lord.'
>   (Collect for Lent 3, ASB)

Opening
doors to
the World
of books

**Book
Tokens**

Book Tokens
can be
bought and
exchanged
at most
bookshops